Sweating the Small Stuff

Sweating the Small Stuff

Answers to Teachers' Big Problems

Joanne C. Wachter

CORWIN PRESS, INC.
A Sage Publications Company
Thousand Oaks, California

For information:

 Corwin Press, Inc.
A Sage Publications Company
2455 Teller Road
Thousand Oaks, California 91320
E-mail: order@corwinpress.com

SAGE Publications Ltd.
6 Bonhill Street
London EC2A 4PU
United Kingdom

SAGE Publications India Pvt. Ltd.
M-32 Market
Greater Kailash I
New Delhi 110 048 India

Printed in the United States of America

Library of Congress Cataloging-in-Publication Data

Wachter, Joanne C.
    Sweating the small stuff: Answers to teachers' big problems /
Joanne C. Wachter.
        p.   cm.
    ISBN 0-8039-6788-8 (cloth: acid-free paper)
    ISBN 0-8039-6789-6 (pbk.: acid-free paper)
    1. Teachers—Handbooks, manuals, etc. 2. Teaching—Handbooks,
manuals, etc.   I. Title.
    LB1775 .S72 1999
    371.102—ddc21   98-40065

This book is printed on acid-free paper.

99 00 01 02 03 04 10 9 8 7 6 5 4 3 2 1

Production Editor: S. Marlene Head
Editorial Assistant: Julia Parnell
Typesetter: Rebecca Evans
Cover Designer: Tracy E. Miller
Cover Photograph by: Comstock, Inc.

Contents

Preface

Teaching is a complicated job. As an educator, you have to juggle the roles of instructor, comforter, referee, builder of self-esteem, adviser to parents, assessor, and more. Upon signing your first teaching contract, you were instantly faced with the need to be an expert in managing all of these responsibilities and the millions of details that each includes. You had to do this after only 4 years of "book learning" and a few months of practice teaching.

Although you may feel very confident about your subject areas, the little details of managing and carrying out the job can trip up any educator, whether novice or veteran. No one has all of the answers to the intricacies of planning, grading, dealing with parents, promoting positive behavior, and the myriad other issues that make teaching a challenge.

Reasons for *Sweating the Small Stuff*

Many books are available on specific elements of teaching, such as classroom management or how to set up hands-on science classrooms. *Sweating the Small Stuff* differs in that it is a survival guide. It gives quick bits of practical advice on the many questions that may come up in implementing a classroom program. After inspiring you with ideas about how to sweat the small stuff related to each topic, it then suggests resources for more in-depth study of the particular challenge you are facing.

Who Will Profit From *Sweating the Small Stuff*?

Sweating the Small Stuff was written primarily with elementary classroom teachers in mind. If you are a beginning teacher or a student teacher, studying the book in depth while considering how to set up your classroom program for the first time will be helpful. If you have been teaching for years, browsing through the book for new ideas or variations on ideas you are already using will be enjoyable.

If you are a principal, assistant principal, coordinator for a beginning teacher program, or central office supervisor, *Sweating the Small Stuff* will also be useful. Consider it as a source of ideas for teachers who need extra support to solve problems. Also, use the book to help successful teachers stay fresh and interested in their programs.

Although some of the ideas in *Sweating the Small Stuff* are written from the elementary classroom perspective, many of the techniques will also interest middle and high school teachers, as well as church school teachers and educators in preschool programs. If you are a substitute teacher or teaching assistant, you will also find many helpful ideas in this book. In addition, *Sweating the Small Stuff* is great for use as a supplementary text for methods classes, particularly in student teaching courses.

How Is *Sweating the Small Stuff* Set Up?

In planning *Sweating the Small Stuff,* major impact areas for classroom teachers were identified. These included topics such as Planning, Implementing Lessons, Assessing and Grading, Handling the Paperwork, Avoiding Burnout, and many other critical issues. For each topic, key questions that teachers frequently ask were brainstormed. These questions came from the author's own experience as an elementary teacher as well as more than 10 years of supervising and coaching veteran and beginning elementary, middle, and high school teachers.

For each question, some practical tips have been given. These ideas can be tried out during the course of a school year. They generally require little time and a minimum of additional "sweat" but can make a big difference in how a classroom program operates. Furthermore, there is a "Try This Today" idea for each question to get you started in solving and preventing problems immediately. Finally, each section contains a collection of references for further reading and study when you want more in-depth information.

Sweating the Small Stuff can be read cover to cover to spark ideas, or it can be used like an emergency first aid book when something in your classroom is not working the way you envisioned and you want a source of new ideas. It is an easy-to-read book that you can take with you for idea browsing during odd moments, such as when you are waiting for a meeting to start.

Acknowledgments

I would like to express appreciation to the many fine teachers from whom I have learned during my 20 or so years as an educator. One aspect of the profession I love is how teachers share, borrow, and build on techniques and strategies until it is usually impossible to identify the originator of an idea. I often tease teachers with whom I work by telling them that good teaching does not rely on creating all of one's own ideas from scratch as much as knowing which ideas are worth stealing from colleagues. I admire the fact that educators take it as a compliment when their ideas are shared and used by others. Therefore, I thank all of the teachers whose ideas are represented in *Sweating the Small Stuff.* I may have written the book, but it would not have been possible to do so without the wonderful opportunity I have each day to observe and brainstorm with master teachers in Carroll County, Maryland. These dedicated educators work their magic with kids by taking time to sweat the small stuff.

I also want to thank the professionals at Corwin Press, who are beginning to feel like friends after having published several of my books. I especially appreciate the enthusiasm of Alice Foster in listening to my ideas and encouraging my writing. I thank Marlene Head for always making my ideas look so good in print as she sweats the small stuff associated with making a book happen.

I thank my readers, who would not be interested in this book if they had not dedicated their minds and hearts to providing the best possible educational experience for the youngsters in their care. Even "okay teaching" takes a tremendous amount of time and effort. Continually striving to sweat the important small stuff is even more admirable.

Finally, I thank my husband Jerry Wachter for his constant support and his enthusiastic encouragement of my writing.

JOANNE C. WACHTER
Baltimore, Maryland
May 1998

About the Author

Joanne C. Wachter has been an educator for more than 20 years, having taught in both public and private elementary schools. She is currently a supervisor working with elementary, middle school, and high school teachers. In that role, she has a chance to visit many schools and work with teachers and administrators on issues ranging from curriculum to classroom management.

In addition to her work in education, her other love is writing. She is the author of more than 50 instructional materials and professional books for teachers. Her most recent works are *Time-Saving Tips for Teachers* (1997, Corwin Press), coauthored with Clare Carhart, and *You Don't Have to Dread Cafeteria Duty: A Guide to Surviving Lunchroom, Recess, Bus, and "Other Duties as Assigned"* (1998, Corwin Press), coauthored with Dori E. Novak.

1
Sweating the Small Stuff

We often hear that we should not "sweat the small stuff," but here is a new thought related to your teaching program: What if you sweated the small stuff in order to prevent big problems?

Sweating the small stuff means putting extra effort into important details. Sweating the small stuff does *not* mean that you need to become obsessed with every tiny aspect. As a matter of fact, just the opposite is true. If you sweat the small stuff, at least the important small stuff, you will reduce your stress because you will avoid most of the big problems that could trip you up.

Why Sweat the Small Stuff?

Remember the old adage, "Take care of the pennies, and the dollars will take care of themselves"? You have no doubt noticed this effect in various aspects of your life. For instance, if you pay attention to seemingly small details like measurements and ingredients, your projects are easier to do and turn out better, whether you are baking a cake or building a bookshelf.

The same result is true for teaching. When you pay attention to the details, your program will be easier to implement, and both you and your children will enjoy it more. This concept applies whether you are planning a unit, getting ready for a parent conference, or grading papers.

Which Small Stuff Is Worth Sweating?

A word of caution is in order. You need to develop the self-discipline to sweat just the important stuff. If you indiscriminantly sweat all stuff, you will cause yourself more problems than you solve. It is critical to sort out the fine points that matter from those that do not and put your sweat into the aspects that count.

How to Sweat the Small Stuff

Once you decide that it might be helpful to sweat the small stuff, how do you go about it? The answer is that you resolve to be open to looking at important details with new eyes. In some cases, this examination of various aspects of teaching may lead you to do some things in a completely new way; in other cases, you may simply try a new twist on an old technique you have already been using.

Sweating the Small Stuff was written to help you think about many elements of teaching and see if you want to make some modifications in your program. Some of the ideas in the book may be ones you want to try, and others may spark a totally new idea in your mind. Browse through this mega-hardware store of teaching ideas and pick out the tools and techniques that fit your style and your youngsters.

2

Setting Up
Your Classroom

Think about your classroom as a home away from home for youngsters in your class. Make it as warm and inviting as possible. The decisions you make in setting up your classroom can have a major impact on your instructional program and children's learning behaviors. Put a lot of thought into decor decisions . . . and have fun with this aspect of teaching.

How Should I Arrange the Desks?

- Consider the kinds of activities youngsters will be asked to do. Will most of their work be individual assignments? Will they need to get into cooperative clusters a lot? Do you need a space for meeting with groups on the floor? Decide how to arrange seating based on the answers to these questions.

- If you incorporate a lot of group work into your program, think about sitting children in clusters so that youngsters will not have to move desks every time you assign a cooperative activity. Groupings of six work best. This provides the flexibility of meeting in pairs, triads, or a group of six.

- Be sure that there is plenty of space to pull out chairs without children bumping into each other.

- If your room is noisy because you have no carpeting, put tennis balls on the ends of chair legs to muffle sound.

- Set up interesting areas in your room, such as a publishing area, a quiet space to think and read, or a place to observe nature. Let your imagination go.

Try This Today

As a warm-up or filler activity, ask children to draw their ideas of possible room arrangements. Collect these and see if they spark any practical ideas.

What Do I Put on All Those Bulletin Boards?

- Use posters, precut letters, and commercially prepared pictures as much as possible to save time.
- Use bulletin boards as a space for resources such as word walls, proofreading symbols, maps, or whatever else is pertinent to your subject area so that your boards are functional as well as decorative.
- Ask parent volunteers to be bulletin board coordinators and artists.
- Designate at least one bulletin board as a place to showcase children's work.
- Decide on a theme for your room. Pick something for which it is easy to find commercially produced materials, such as a circus theme or a regional theme. Building your bulletin board and other decorations around a central idea will make it easier to come up with ideas. Also, if you let parents know about your theme, they may share or make materials to help you decorate bulletin boards and other areas.
- Consider using one or more of your bulletin board areas as celebration spaces to recognize children for individual and group successes. These accomplishments can be related to achievement in the classroom or in the community. Elicit children's help in adorning these spots with balloons, streamers, and other festive touches.

Try This Today

Get children involved in designing and creating bulletin boards. Hang up a "help wanted" poster outside your door to recruit either children from your class or older youngsters.

Where Do I Put Supplies?

- Put supplies in cupboards and on shelves as much as possible so that they do not cause visual clutter. Label doors to cupboards so that you and the children know where everything is at a glance.
- Get inexpensive, colorful plastic bins to store materials that you may need to be portable, such as art supplies, math manipulatives, and writing tools.
- Store resources such as dictionaries, spell checkers, and other references in places where children can get them independently and without causing a classroom traffic jam.

Try This Today

Look at your room. Decide on three things you could move to make them either more accessible or out of the way depending on how often you need the items. Give yourself a peace-of-mind gift by moving them right now.

How Can I Manage the Classroom Library?

- Get the children involved in thinking with you about how the library corner can be made cozy and comfortable. For instance, you might want to invite some stuffed animals to live there.
- Arrange your books by genre so that you and the children can more easily find particular kinds of books.
- Teach several children how to put away books in your classroom library so that they can act as your library assistants.
- Increase your library by getting books from book clubs, yard sales, and donations from parents of books their children have outgrown. You might undertake this as a schoolwide project so that books of various levels can be collected and sorted among the grades.
- In the library, also include books, stories, and articles your children have "published."
- Get a rubber stamp with your name and the school's name on it. Ask some children from your class or from older classes, or ask parent volunteers to stamp each book in your library to make it easy to sort your books from those that the children may bring in from their own collections.

- If you do not have adequate bookshelves, use inexpensive plastic bins turned on their sides and stacked. As an alternative, sturdy cardboard boxes can be decorated and used in the same way. The decorations might illustrate the kinds of books shelved in each box.
- Develop a simple sign-out system for books that the children wish to take home. One way to handle this is to find a parent volunteer who will paste a pocket in each book, as well as make a card with the title on it and lines where a child can sign his or her name and the date the book is taken.

Name	Title	Date Taken	Return Date
Mark	*Stone Fox*	Sept. 16	Sept. 23

Figure 2.1. Sample Library Card Sign-Out

 Try This Today

Identify one of your parent volunteers, or ask in the office to see if there is a volunteer willing to be responsible for overseeing your classroom library. He or she might find inexpensive or free sources of additional materials, devise a shelving system, and maintain the checkout system for take-home books.

What Do I Do When I Have Too Many Kids and Too Little Space?

- Consolidate by arranging the children's desks in clusters rather than rows so that they take up less space.
- Put your desk in the back of the room with just enough space behind it to comfortably fit your chair.
- Put as many items up on shelves and on the wall as possible so that you are not wasting floor space.

■ Collect pillows and carpet squares so that children can spread out on the floor for reading, group sharing, and other activities that do not require a desk surface.

Try This Today

Talk to the children about the space problem and get their good ideas about how you can arrange furniture, manage traffic patterns, and interact with each other so that the space situation is more comfortable.

How Do I Keep My Classroom Looking Neat and Feeling Comfortable?

■ Recruit an Environment Team to straighten your room at the end of each day. You might want to elevate the importance of this role by having children fill out simple application forms telling which aspects of the environment (chalkboards, bookshelves, computer area, and so on) they would like to manage and why they think they would do a good job. Some type of recognition can be given periodically.

■ From time to time, announce a Good Housekeeping Contest to help children be conscious of maintaining a pleasant, orderly environment. Establish contest rules, such as determining that a certain number of points will be the goal for the week. Determine what neatness behaviors will earn the points, and award the appropriate number to each cluster of desks or row at the end of each day. All of the groups who meet the goal at the end of the week can be awarded a little prize or treat.

	Points Earned				
	Row 1	*Row 2*	*Row 3*	*Row 4*	*Row 5*
Desks neatly placed					
Paper scraps thrown away					
Materials neatly stored in desks					

Figure 2.2. Good Housekeeping Contest

- Make a Neat Class bulletin board or poster. Whenever you or someone else notices one of your children doing something to add to the classroom environment, fill out a little note and attach it to the display. At the end of the week, each child can take home his or her notes, and the process can start over the next week.

```
Dear Pat,

Thanks for helping me clean up when we spilled the paint
yesterday. I appreciate your efforts at making our room
look nice again.
```

Figure 2.3. Sample Neatness Note

- Who says your classroom has to look the way classrooms have looked for decades? Be creative about furnishings. Never turn down any old cushions, lamps, rockers, or other homey touches that are offered to you. Think of yard sales as your interior decorator warehouses.
- Consider the use of background music during reading, writing, and other quiet work times. Stick to peaceful, restful mood pieces.
- Experiment with aromas in your classroom. For example, orange is supposed to be calmly invigorating, whereas lavender is supposed to soothe stress. Have your children read about aromatherapy and experiment with different scents to see if they have a positive effect on atmosphere and productivity.

 Try This Today

Take a moment at the end of each class to ask children to pick up anything that has fallen on the floor.

For More Ideas and Information . . .

- Take a tour of your school. Notice the room arrangements being used by colleagues. If you find any that are appealing, ask why the room was set up this way, how it is working, and if there are any pitfalls.

- Take a tour of a large office supply store, or look in a catalog. Focus on taking a creative look at the kinds of storage options available, and think about how you could use them.

- Talk to your school media specialist about his or her ideas for classroom libraries.

- Find out whether any of the parents in your class or school is an interior designer. Ask him or her for ideas about how you can maximize your space.

- Read *Bulletin Boards for Every Month* by Jeanne and Arnold Cheyney (Scott Foresman).

- Look at *Literature-Based Bulletin Boards* by Elizabeth Shelton Wollner and Sharon Rodgers, and *Flip-up Bulletin Boards* by Muriel Feldhub (Scholastic Books, 1-800-724-6527).

- Get *Bulletin Boards for Reinforcing Positive Behavior* (Canter and Associates, 1-800-262-4347).

3
Planning

Planning is one secret to being an outstanding teacher. When you take time to think through how you will present instruction, your youngsters will learn more easily and you will enjoy teaching.

How Do I Write Objectives, Outcomes, or Goals?

■ Think of not only what children will do but why. (Example: Children will learn to identify subjects and predicates so that they can discriminate between sentences and sentence fragments.)

■ Put often-used objectives on sentence strips and laminate these. Hang them with magnets and store for use from year to year so that you do not have to copy them on the board each day.

Objective: Students will begin sentences with capitals and end them with ending punctuation.

Figure 3.1. Sentence Strip Objective

■ Cut overhead transparencies into strips and put objectives on them with permanent marker. Put the appropriate one(s) on the overhead at the beginning of class to focus children's attention.

Try This Today

Decide on a place where you will store objective strips. Make a file or clean out the space before you leave today.

How Do I Create Long-Range Plans?

■ Consider sketching out your intentions for units on a timeline.

Sept/Oct	Nov/Dec	Jan/Feb	Mar/Apr
Insects	Sink or float	Weather	Plant growth

Figure 3.2. Science Unit Timeline

■ Meet with other teachers at your grade level to collaborate on ideas and materials for units.

■ Create a mind-map or a web of all the units you need and want to fit in during the year. List some of the key elements to cover and activities under each. Go back and decide on the order in which you will address the clusters.

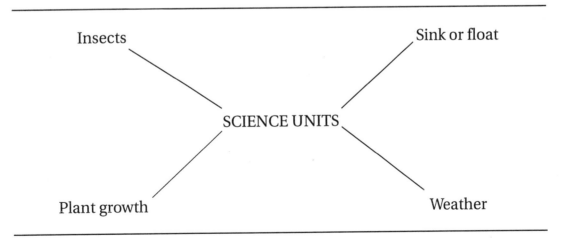

Figure 3.3. Science Unit Web

Try This Today

Keep a folder for each unit that you will teach during the year. As you think of ideas or find materials, slip them into the appropriate folder.

How Do I Approach Daily Plans?

- Experiment with various formats until you find one that fits your style. Consider commercially prepared planning books, handmade forms, and computer calendar formats, along with any other variation that helps you plan efficiently.

- Think of your lessons as having a beginning, middle, and end, just like a story. Consider what you want to accomplish in each part, and then decide which activities you will use to meet your goals.

- See if you can create a fill-in-the-blank format that you will use for each subject area. Reproduce the form in quantity and then fill in the blanks for items such as objectives, materials, steps, homework, and so on. You can use these forms not only for day-to-day planning but also to create substitute plans. Furthermore, take a few forms with you whenever you go to a professional development activity or read a journal so that you can jot down lesson ideas. See Figure 3.4 for a sample substitute planning frame.

- As often as possible, plan with a colleague who teaches your grade. Grab a cup of tea and meet in your workroom, classroom, or a corner of the media center to share the work of planning. It will be more fun, and you can springboard from each other's ideas.

Objective: Children will read a story and expand their comprehension of the story by predicting, responding to high-level-thought questions, and developing vocabulary.

MATERIALS

____ **Book** _____

____ **Story on page** _____ **of the following book** _____

____ **Prediction Sheet** (Before copying the sheet, fill in the number of a page near the middle and near the end that would make reasonable stopping points for predictions)

____ **Thinking Sheet** (If you wish to assign certain items, check these on the master before copying)

____ **Vocabulary Sheet**

____ **Substitute Teacher Response Form**

BEFORE READING

1. Hand out the Prediction Sheet to each child.

2. Direct students to look at the cover or, if the story is in an anthology, the first page.

3. Give them time to fill out the first prediction. (If you are working with primary-grade children, this step can be done orally, or you can record their ideas on a chart paper.)

4. Have several volunteers share the first prediction.

DURING READING

1. Explain to the children that they will be stopping at two other points to make predictions. Point out the page numbers. (If working with primary-grade children, you read with them to the middle prediction point and then, as a group, discuss their predictions before reading to the end.)

Figure 3.4. Substitute Planning Frame—Reading a Short Story

SOURCE: Joanne C. Strohmer and Clare Carhart, *Time-Saving Tips for Teachers* (1997, Corwin Press), p. 81.

Try This Today

Avoid daily planning as your strategy for daily planning! Always plan a week's worth of lessons at a time. You won't have to "look forward" to planning every night, and you will save time by gathering your thoughts and materials one time instead of five times. At the end of classes each day, simply review your plans for the next day and see what minor revisions you might have to make.

What Are Some Ways I Can Build Variety Into My Lessons?

- Use a planning format that encourages you to think about varying activities.

TABLE 3.1 Planning Format

Lesson:

Objective	*Activity*	*Materials*	*Time*
Retell Chapter 3 of *Henry & Beezus*.	Share with your small group.	Copies of the book	2 minutes
Predict what will happen in Chapter 4.	Fill out prediction chart, then whole-class sharing.	Prediction charts	10 minutes
Read to confirm their predictions.	Read with partner or alone—children's choice.	Copies of the book	15 minutes
Compare a character's actions to their own.	Journal entry—How are Henry and you alike?	Journals	10 minutes

- Brainstorm a list of ways that children can respond and practice: group discussion, acting out, partner reading, drawing, journal entries, and so on. Laminate the list and keep it in your planning book as a reminder.
- Offer children a choice of two ways to practice a skill sometimes. For example, give them the option of writing a paragraph or making an illustration with a caption to explain a science project.

- Change the order of some classroom activities. For instance, do a mini-lesson at the end of Writer's Workshop instead of at the beginning, or have children answer the questions in a social studies text, then read the chapter, then add information to their original responses.

- Think of instructional plans as road maps. They give you an idea of where you are going so that you can travel efficiently and get where you intended to go. On the other hand, use these maps flexibly so that you can work around obstacles and avoid the boredom of traveling the same route all the time.

 Try This Today

After you have finished a particular lesson, ask the children to brainstorm some other ways they could have practiced the skill. Jot down any good ideas to apply to future lessons.

How Do I Figure Out How Much Time to Allow for Certain Lessons or Parts of Lessons?

- Survey your colleagues regarding how long they allow for certain kinds of activities.

- Mentally run through the activity yourself, then allow children twice the time it took you.

- Remember that it is much better to run out of time than to run out of activities. Plan a little more than you think children can do. You can always continue the lesson the next day.

- Plan ahead what you will add if children do finish early. For instance, you might create an extra challenge related to your basic lesson by extending it for faster learners. Be sure that the extension is motivating, or youngsters may slow down to avoid doing more work.

- Make notes on your lesson plans (after implementing them) regarding how much time the components actually took so that you will have this information if you file the plan for later reference.

✔ *Try This Today*

Brainstorm with your class some acceptable activities to do whenever they have extra time. (For example, they might read, write in their journals, visit the math puzzle center, and so on.) Post these ideas on a classroom chart or bulletin board for easy reference.

How Do I Incorporate the Use of Technology Into My Program?

- Be on the lookout for ways that you can use technology to make the record-keeping and "administrivia" of your job easier. For example, put forms and parent letters that you use regularly on the computer.

- Search the Internet for the many sites that include lesson plans and other teaching ideas. Make an agreement with a colleague at your grade level or subject area to share what each of you finds so that you will get double the ideas for your effort. *Warning!* Be very critical and selective about the ideas you take from the Internet. Some are great, but others are not worth the cyberspace they take up.

- Set a time limit for yourself when you are "surfing" the Net, or you will find it easy to let the computer gobble up too much of your planning time.

- Also, be very selective about the software you choose for your youngsters to use. If a program does not closely and easily fit into your program, don't use it just because the software is available.

- Learn from the children. They probably know a lot more about computer use than you do.

- At the beginning of the year, survey students to find out how many have computers that they can use at home. Send the parents of these children a letter letting them know that it is okay for homework and other writing assignments to be done on a home computer. Why shouldn't you get papers that are easy to read so that your grading will go faster?

- Why not take a technology course or workshop? These classes can be fun, and they will make you feel more secure.

Try This Today

Make it a goal to ask three colleagues who use the computer what they have found to be the most useful applications. Pick out one or two of these that sound interesting, and ask the person to tell you more or to show you how this application works.

For More Ideas and Information . . .

■ Collect sample unit plans from three colleagues. Review each to see if you can find one new idea to add to how you plan units.

■ Read *Designing Places for Learning,* edited by Anne Meek (Association for Supervision and Curriculum Development, 1-800-933-ASCD).

■ Skim *Language Arts Mini-Lessons* for ideas (Scholastic Books, 1-800-724-6527).

■ Read *Creating and Sustaining the Constructivist Classroom* by Bruce A. Marlowe and Marilyn L. Page (Corwin Press, 1-805-499-9734).

■ Check out *Cooperative Learning: Getting Started Grades K-6* (Scholastic Books, 1-800-724-6527).

■ Get a copy of *Methods That Really Matter* by Harvey Daniels and Marilyn Bizar (Stenhouse, 1-800-988-9812).

■ Subscribe to *Curriculum/Technology Quarterly* (Association for Supervision and Curriculum Development, 1-800-933-ASCD).

■ Check out *Web Feet: The Internet Traveler's Desk Reference,* a monthly guide to best sites (1-800-ROCKHILL).

4
Implementing Lessons

Teaching an effective lesson to a whole class of exuberant learners can be tricky. There are many techniques that can help you manage—and even enjoy—the complex challenge of providing high-quality instruction.

How Do I Get My Class Settled for a Good Start of the Day or Period?

- Start class activities promptly so that children do not have time to even think about getting off task. Convey the attitude that you have a lot of exciting things to share with the youngsters and you do not want to waste a precious moment.

- Establish the routine of having children get ready for the next subject by copying the objectives for the day into their notebooks.

- Find a book or calendar that has inspirational sayings. Put one of these on an overhead transparency each day. Ask children to react by writing a journal entry about what the quote means to them. Younger children could respond with a drawing. If you and a colleague undertake this collaboratively, each of you has to find only half as many.

- Provide a question that children can react to with a journal entry. Consider whether you also want to give them the option of choosing their own topic if they are not motivated by the one you have selected.

- Get children into the habit of lining up outside your classroom and waiting for you to tell them what they will need to do when they enter the room.

■ Have children start to collect their thoughts about what they already know as an opening activity while everyone is gathering. For example, you could ask them to list all the words they can think of that have the prefix "re" if that is what you plan to teach that day.

✓ ### Try This Today

Provide a puzzle or brainteaser on an overhead or chart paper for children to do before class starts. File and save these puzzles for use from year to year.

What Are Effective Teaching Practices?

■ Refer back to the objectives at various points of the lesson. Ask children to identify to which objective a certain activity connects. Remind them of why they are doing specific tasks.

■ Keep teacher talk to a minimum. Children will learn more if they are expected to respond and be active than if they just listen to you.

■ Expect your class to involve noise and movement sometimes. Animated discussion and responsible movement around the room can be signs of a productive classroom.

■ Provide an actual planned closure. Sure, you have heard that a million times, but it is so easy to let the clock get away from you. Consider, however, that the last moments of class are what children will remember most according to learning theory. Don't throw away those precious moments. Ask for volunteers to tell you what they learned.

■ Balance your lesson plan with the need to accommodate your learners. It is okay to change on the spot if your youngsters are not having success or if they are showing you that they already know what you are attempting to teach.

■ Use logic and your persuasive powers to convince children of the importance of what you are asking them to do. Challenge yourself to explain in believable terms how they will use what you are teaching in real life. For instance, tell children that you are teaching them about subjects and predicates so that they will have a way to check whether they are writing complete sentences when they express their ideas in writing.

- Don't use your desk while the children are in your classroom! Be a teacher who is constantly moving around your room. Even if children are all working on an independent project, use the time to circulate, coach, and encourage.
- Sit among the children sometimes and do the assignment on which they are working.

Try This Today

Begin each subject by taking a moment to discuss the lesson objective with the class. For instance, a child can be asked to read the objective from the board or overhead. In order to foster interest, youngsters can be invited to tell why they think you selected that objective or what they already know about the subject or skill to be addressed.

What Do I Do to Get Kids Excited About My Lesson?

- Find ways to connect everything you teach to the children and their lives. Start with what they already know and make clear to them how learning more about the topic or skill will help them in life outside the classroom. For example, learning math operations could be connected to operating a lemonade stand, or reading about pollution could be connected with cleaning up a stream in their community.
- Incorporate themes, characters, current events, and topics that are interesting to children. For example, you could use a baseball theme for a reading incentive program in the spring.
- Keep children actively involved rather than expecting them to listen for long periods of time. Stop at strategic points and have youngsters pair up and share on a specific question related to what you are teaching. For example, if you have just presented information about Japanese culture, ask youngsters to turn to the child next to them and share three ways in which Japanese culture is different from American culture.
- Change activities often, and balance quiet with active tasks.

Try This Today

Consciously try to introduce lessons with excitement in your voice and a twinkle in your eye.

How Do I Decide Whether to Have Kids Work in Groups or Individually?

- If youngsters have been engaged in whole-class or individual work, a period of group work may provide needed variety.
- Use group work if that approach would help youngsters learn more. For instance, if your class is studying a certain culture, having each small group research a particular aspect (education, geography, resources, and so on) and then present to each other would be an efficient way to learn more.
- If youngsters need to read material that may be challenging for some of them, having children read with partners is a valid strategy.
- Consider the purpose of the task. If it is for individual assessment, youngsters should work individually.

Try This Today

Once in awhile, after you introduce an activity, ask children whether they think they would learn more working individually or in small groups. Have them defend their ideas and use their input.

How Do I Make Group Work Worthwhile and Productive?

- Be sure that youngsters clearly understand what they are to do before you have them start the task. Take some time to have children verbalize back to you the expectations.
- If appropriate, ask a group to model what they are to do so that others can watch before attempting the task.
- Consider how to group children. Random groupings may be fine for short activities within a single class period. More purposeful group assignments might be needed for major, long-term projects.

- Assign roles such as recorder, encourager, materials handler, or whatever other roles would make work more efficient. Be explicit about what each role involves.

- Structure the work so that everyone contributes ideas to a group project rather than one or two children coming up with ideas that others copy onto their papers. For example, provide children with one handout with a question such as, "What do you predict will happen in the next chapter of our read-aloud and why?" Have each contribute an idea and initial it. Have all group members who agree with each prediction initial it in a different color than the one used by the person who generated the idea.

- Create a simple group work self-evaluation. Take a moment for groups to discuss it as they finish their assigned task.

Did Our Group . . . ?

_____ Stick to the topic

_____ Include everyone in the conversation

_____ Respect everyone's ideas

_____ Finish our task

Overall:

_____ We did a great job.   _____ We need to work harder.

Figure 4.1. Sample Group Work Self-Evaluation

Try This Today

Put directions for group work on an overhead or chart paper, and go over them orally as well. This will help both your visual and auditory learners remember what to do. Keep the visual reminder up throughout the group activity so that youngsters can refresh their memories.

How Do I Handle Transitions Smoothly?

- Use a hand sign or flick of the lights to signal time for a transition. Train youngsters to stop and listen for directions.

- Provide a visual or auditory cue to let children know 5 minutes in advance of the end of an activity. This warning will help them tie up loose ends and mentally prepare for a change of task.

- Tell children that they have a certain number of minutes to make the transition you have described. Set a timer and see if everyone can meet the goal.

- Assign one child to watch the clock and time how long it takes for a transition. Record the time on a corner of the board or chart. See if youngsters can improve their time. Provide verbal reinforcement and rewards for progress.

Try This Today

Ask one child to be a process observer during a transition. Have the child be on the lookout for three things the class did well and one goal for improvement. Remind them of the goal just before the next transition opportunity.

For More Ideas and Information . . .

- Read the series *From Knowing to Showing* by Helen L. Burz and Kit Marshall (*Performance-Based Curriculum for Mathematics, Performance-Based Curriculum for Language Arts, Performance-Based Curriculum for Science,* and *Performance-Based Curriculum for Social Studies,* Corwin Press, 1-805-499-9734).

- Use the resource *Teaching Reading, Writing, and Spelling* by Virginia Talbot (Corwin, 1-805-499-9734).

- Ask one of the most seasoned teachers in your school what tricks for smooth transitions she or he has discovered over the years.

- Look at *Unbelievably Good Deals That You Simply Can't Get Unless You're a Teacher* by Barry Harrington and Beth Christensen (Contemporary Books).

5
Promoting Positive Behavior

For youngsters to get the most out of your well-planned, interesting lessons, they must practice productive behaviors. Children are not born knowing how to behave in a classroom setting. They need lots of support and encouragement from you.

How Do I Establish Classroom Rules?

- State rules in positive terms. Tell what you want children to do, not what you do not want.

- Do not overwhelm children with lots of rules. Stick to a few important ones.

- Involve youngsters in making class rules on the first day of school. Have them tell you what rules they think would support a peaceful classroom atmosphere. Add your own if you feel there are any important omissions.

- Present rules that were used by your class last year (or by a colleague's class). Engage the children in revising the rules to meet their particular class's needs.

- Show youngsters several sets of rules. Have small groups discuss which set they feel is most important for the class to adopt and explain why.

- When a set of rules has been agreed upon, have individuals sign behavior agreement contracts.

- Send copies of your class rules home to parents and ask for their support in promoting these behaviors.

- Create a signal to use when you need your whole group to get quiet and attend to your directions or instruction. Teach children the signal, such as raising your hand, ringing a little bell, or holding up a stop sign. Have them practice responding to it. Consider noting on a corner of the board or a chart how much time it takes for them to respond, and challenge them to keep improving their time.
- Show appreciation for productive behavior by making positive comments about certain individuals or groups, providing occasional surprises for individuals or groups who are on task, or sending positive notes home.

 Try This Today

Consider what you will call the behaviors you want to promote: rules, guidelines, class agreements. Think about the connotations and tone of each. Get children involved in pondering this question, if you wish.

How Can I Help Kids Keep the Rules?

- Post the rules.
- Speak to children privately about their behavior. Embarrassing them in front of their peers will only make them act out more in the long run.
- In general, consistency in applying rules is important. However, it is also critical to honor individual differences and needs. Sometimes, this may lead to varying your application of consequences. For instance, if a certain child frequently distracts others, you may handle the situation more firmly than with a child who is generally responsible but slips once. Be open with the children about these situations and explain the reasons for your decisions.
- When someone's behavior is problematic, ask him or her what rule is being broken, and discuss the reasons and remedies.
- Provide surprise rewards for productive behavior. For instance, you could announce, "The green group did such a good job this morning that they may line up first to go to the cafeteria, and I am going to let each member of the group choose a candy to take to lunch." Not being able to predict when good behavior will get rewarded will keep your youngsters on their toes.

- Work toward a class reward for productive behavior. Put up a chart that lists points for certain behaviors. Add points every time they are earned. When a predetermined goal is reached, give the class their reward.

TABLE 5.1   Behavior Points

| *Good Work!* | | | | |
Productive Behaviors	*Points*			
Got settled quickly	0	1	2	3
Stayed on task during class discussion	0	1	2	3
Worked well in groups	0	1	2	3
Followed directions for cleanup	0	1	2	3

- Get a sign language book and teach your children signs for words and phrases such as *stop, quiet, sit down,* and *line up.* Use these as fun ways to give directions.

- Get a few small stuffed animals or figurines to be "desk friends." Occasionally, put these on the tables of children who are doing a good job with productive behaviors. If a child has gotten off task, his or her token can be temporarily removed and placed on someone else's desk. Once in awhile, those who have the token on their desks at the end of class can be given a surprise treat. Other times, just let having this "friend" on their desk for a while be the reward.

- As an alternative to the desk friend strategy, print up coupons to award to children who are showing productive behaviors. Again, on a random pattern, those who have coupons at the end of class can be given a little reward or treat.

- Establish consequences for breaking the rules. Be sure the consequences are related to the rules. For example, if a child is breaking a rule about staying on task and doing his or her work, ask the child to move to a more private place in the room so that he or she will be less likely to be distracted.

- Consider that a child who is acting out may be doing so because he or she feels defeated as a result of attempting assignments that are beyond him or her. Try adjusting the difficulty level and see if the child becomes more cooperative.

- Remember the power of gentle humor to remind children of expectations without being unpleasant.

✔ *Try This Today*

Commit to sending one positive note a day or three notes at the end of each week to let parents know about good behavior. You can create a little form or postcard to make the process efficient. Send the first note today.

When Should I Call Parents About Behavior and What Should I Say?

- Do not hesitate to call parents about unacceptable behavior. It is better for the child to learn immediately that you are serious about productive behavior, and parents would prefer to hear about a problem when it is small rather than when it has become major.

- Up front, let the parent know you are calling because you care about the child and want him or her to do well. Recognize that this is what parents want, too.

- Tell the parent matter of factly what the child's behavior has been and what it needs to be. Be caring but direct. If you are too subtle, the message may be missed altogether.

- Ask the parent if she or he has any idea if there is anything troubling the child that could be leading to the behavior.

- Communicate to the parent an idea you are going to try. See if she or he thinks it will work. Ask for other ideas.

- Try to come up with a solution that involves both you and the parent. For example, you could send home a little check-off form to tell how the child works each day or week and have the parent sign it. Rewards could be given for improvement.

- Get the guidance counselor's or school psychologist's ideas about how to talk to parents concerning problems. Maybe your administrator could ask the counselor to present a faculty meeting session on this topic.

- Involve someone else, such as the principal, if you have talked to the parent and do not feel that your communication is helping.

Try This Today

Turn the tables. When a child has difficulty behaving productively, call his or her parents and say that you would like the child to stay after school. Instead of involving the child in some punishment, have him or her help you with a project, such as putting up a bulletin board. Talk with the youngster about the problem, and also just get to know the child and let him or her get to know you a bit. Sometimes, this will change a child's attitude.

How Do I Promote Positive Behavior During Lunch and Recess?

- Try to keep as positive an attitude as possible. Remember, these times are only a brief part of your whole day.

- Use some techniques to try to encourage the children's cooperation. For instance, handle problems without embarrassing children, and thank them for good efforts.

- Try positive reinforcement. Occasionally plan a treat, such as being able to go out to play 5 minutes early the next day for groups that do an especially nice job in the cafeteria or on the playground. The teacher who has recess duty may be willing to go out early if you reciprocate by doing the same for him or her sometimes.

- Work with your administrator and other teachers to see if you can undertake positive efforts to improve cafeteria and recess experiences. For instance, you might establish some schoolwide expectations for how cafeteria "patrons" behave and elicit everyone's support in posting and upholding these standards.

- See if you can find a little space in the cafeteria to use for a time-out table for youngsters who are having trouble on a particular day. Do not be heavy-handed and bill this as a punishment table but simply a place where a child can regain his or her composure and then try going back to sitting with peers.

- Teach children some positive, collaborative games they can play at recess.

- Ask parents early in the year to donate board games that can be played quietly during indoor recess, or find some at yard sales. Keep these games for use only during inclement weather recess so that their novelty does not wear off.
- Provide several centers for indoor recreation. These might include the reading corner, a drawing area, and a math puzzle center.

Try This Today

For a warm-up activity, have children write a journal entry about what they enjoy and don't enjoy about their time either in the cafeteria or on the playground. Collect these, and then over a period of days, share some (with the author's permission) and engage children in discussions of how these times could be improved.

For More Ideas and Information . . .

- Read *You Don't Have to Dread Cafeteria Duty* by Dori Novak and Joanne C. Strohmer (Corwin Press, 1-805-499-9734).
- Read *The Caring Teacher's Guide to Discipline* by Marilyn E. Gootman (Corwin Press, 1-805-499-9734).
- Take a look at *Teaching Students to Get Along* by Lee Canter and Katia Petersen (Lee Canter and Associates, 1-800-262-4347).
- Look for ideas in *The Unmotivated Child* by Natalie Rathvon (Simon and Schuster).
- Study *Success With Challenging Students* by Jeffrey A. Kottler (Corwin Press, 1-805-499-9734).
- Check *Teaching Conflict Resolution Through Children's Literature* by William Kreidler (Scholastic, 1-800-724-6527).
- Study *Discipline With Dignity* by Richard Curwin and Allen Mendler (Association for Supervision and Curriculum Development, 1-800-933-ASCD).
- Use *Positive Reinforcement Activities* (Canter and Associates, 1-800-262-4347).

6

Handling Student Speeches, Projects, and Presentations

A high-quality program includes a wide variety of ways for children to learn. Speeches, projects, and presentations can add spice and pizzazz to the classroom routine. These events can also add special challenges for you, so planning and implementation strategies are important.

What Kinds of Projects Are Worthwhile to Assign?

- Create projects that are closely tied to the learning objectives. For instance, a diorama about a book the child is reading may not tell you much about comprehension. On the other hand, having to write a paragraph explaining the significance to the book of the diorama scene enhances the learning.

- Assign projects that build in choices for youngsters. Provide a balance of tasks that allow outgoing children as well as quieter learners to be successful.

- Projects that involve family members help establish good home-school relationships. A side benefit is that some of the nonacademic work involved, such as building models or collecting and putting together materials for costumes, can be done without using up class time.

- Provide balanced projects that use multiple intelligences, such as musical, artistic, and athletic talents.

■ Projects, speeches, and presentations are natural opportunities for teaching collaborative skills by having children work in pairs or small groups.

 Try This Today

On a section of your chalkboard or a piece of chart paper, write the title of one of your next units. Tell the children a bit about this "upcoming attraction." Ask them to think of projects that might provide interesting ways to show what they learn about the topic. Invite them to jot these down when they have a moment during the next few days. See if you can use some of their ideas in the unit.

How Do I Schedule Presentations?

■ Schedule presentations or speeches a few at a time so that you do not lose major chunks of class time. For instance, three or four children a day could present their social studies projects at the beginning of social studies class for each of several days.

■ Let the children have some say in how presentations are scheduled. Some youngsters may wish to go first and get it over with, whereas others may need to see some classmates go first so that they can get a perspective on what is expected and also build up their confidence.

■ For projects, consider having a museum day, gallery walk, or other event that lays out all of the projects and provides time for children and possibly other visitors to view all of the work at once in a confined time period.

■ Break children into triads or quads. Have each child present his or her project, speech, or other presentation to the small group. All groups can work simultaneously so that lots of presentations can take place in a short time.

Try This Today

Presentations can be sprinkled throughout the day. For example, one or two youngsters could give their speech or project at the beginning of the day, a couple could present before lunch and a few more after lunch, and then a few could present at the end of the day.

What Can I Do to Keep the Audience Attentive When Students Are Presenting Speeches or Projects?

- Conduct a mini-lesson before the presentations start. Help youngsters recall the kinds of behaviors that mature audiences demonstrate. Chart their ideas, and hang these in a visible place during the presentations. At strategic points or at the end, have children self-evaluate using the chart.

- Give each child a peer evaluation sheet that has several ideas or behaviors to look for during the presentations or speeches. Have the audience fill out these sheets after the presentation.

- If you use a museum or gallery format for showing off projects, ask half of the youngsters to stand by their work so that the rest of the class can visit the exhibits and ask questions of the creators. After all have had a chance to visit the exhibits, switch and let the other half of the children stand by their work.

- Give children a checklist of things to find when they are visiting a display of classmates' projects.

Try This Today

Once in a while, use an "Imagine This" project approach. Give youngsters group time to draw or write a description of a model, video, or other project to apply a concept you are teaching. For example, have them tell or illustrate what materials they would use and how they would construct a weathervane when you are studying wind. Going through this process will help children grapple with concepts without taking up major periods of time for construction and presentation.

For More Ideas and Information . . .

- Check out *New Curriculum for New Times* by Neal A. Glasgow (Corwin Press, 1-805-499-9734).
- Read *Developing Students' Multiple Intelligences* by Kristen Nicholson (Scholastic, 1-800-724-6527).
- Get a copy of *Better Than Book Reports* by Christine Boardman Moen (Scholastic, 1-800-724-6527).

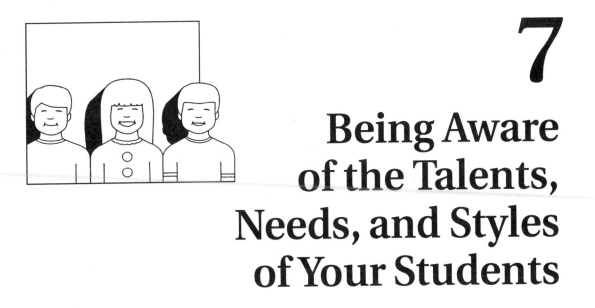

7

Being Aware of the Talents, Needs, and Styles of Your Students

Your class is made up of a combination of unique individuals. Each has special strengths and needs. If that were not enough of a challenge, the youngsters in your class also vary in their learning styles. Instead of shaking your sanity, this diversity can be reason for celebration if you handle the situation with effective techniques.

How Do I Deal With Variations in Reading Pace?

- Get children involved in setting goals for how many pages they will read in a specified amount of time. If they participate in this decision, it may be more realistic, and they will also feel more motivated to meet a deadline if they have helped set it.
- Use partner reading sometimes as a way to speed up the pace.
- Be realistic about the level of reading that individuals can handle. Provide easier materials for slower readers so that they can keep up.
- Of course, in reading class, youngsters need to do their own reading so that they can acquire skills. In other subjects, such as social studies or science,

you can use a listening station sometimes. Have parent volunteers or fluent children from upper grades tape passages, which you can then use year after year.

✔ *Try This Today*

Break your class into groups of three or four. Assign one child to be the reading leader. (Pick a fluent reader.) Have the others echo along as the leader reads.

What Do I Do About Children Who Write Slowly?

- Beg, borrow, and . . . um . . . do whatever you can to get as many computers as possible in your room. Let children for whom writing is laborious use them frequently.

- Once children have learned both manuscript and cursive, give them a choice of using whichever is most efficient for them when you can. Of course, they need some ongoing practice with both forms so that they do not lose either skill.

- Do some kid watching (or ask your reading specialist, parent volunteer, or someone else) to discover specific reasons that a particular child writes slowly. Is it laborious letter formation, awkward posture, a physical problem? Use your own ideas and those of colleagues to help the child remedy or compensate for the problem.

- If children are having problems copying from the board efficiently, provide a mini-lesson to show them how to look at phrases. Teach them how to hold phrases in their heads so that they do not have to look up for every word or, worse yet, every letter.

- Try to notice if some children are having a problem writing because they have a hard time getting ideas rather than because of a handwriting problem. With these youngsters, use writing fluency exercises often. For instance, have them freewrite whatever ideas come to their heads (even if it is, "I can't think of anything to write!") without lifting their pens from the paper. Start with a small amount of time. Gradually increase it as they become more confident.

Try This Today

See if using a different writing implement makes writing easier for an individual who writes with difficulty. Compare pencil to pen, fine point to medium, felt tip to ballpoint, fat pen to skinny, and so on to see what helps.

How Can I Accommodate Children's Different Learning Styles?

- Provide a choice of ways to respond to assignments sometimes. For instance, let children choose between writing a paragraph, creating a graphic organizer, or making an illustration with a caption to show their comprehension of a reading selection or video.
- Present directions in both written and oral form.
- Use diagrams, pictures, and other graphics in addition to verbal descriptions and explanations of concepts.
- Use projects from time to time as a teaching approach. Projects can integrate various learning modes, including discussing, building, drawing, writing, reading, and others.
- Use cooperative learning groups, and divide roles and responsibilities according to children's strengths.
- Offer children a choice sometimes between working alone or collaboratively.
- Provide different kinds of environments in which to work within your room. For instance, include sections with desks grouped together, a few desks off to the side, and cushions or carpet squares for informal work spaces. Provide mini-lessons and chart expectations to help children know how to work productively in different settings.

Try This Today

Talk with children about what helps them work and what distracts them. As a class, brainstorm ways to enhance their work areas to support them in being productive.

What Do I Do When a Child Is Having Problems Learning?

- Talk to the child. See if she or he is aware of the problem and can shed some light on the reason for it. Start this private conversation by reminding the child that you want him or her to be successful, and you are willing to help in any way.

- Check the child's records to see if you can find any clues about how to help him or her be successful.

- Contact the child's parents; sooner is better than later. Ask what the parents are noticing. See if they know of anything that could be distracting or distressing the child.

- Talk to other teachers who work with the child and to previous teachers, if possible. Find out what they have discovered that works.

- Experiment with modifying assignments to see if the child is more successful when asked to study or respond in a different way.

- Try an incentive program to motivate the child's interest and effort.

- Find an older child or a parent volunteer who is willing to provide one-on-one coaching to help the child learn skills and gain confidence.

- Talk to support people, such as reading specialists, guidance counselors, and some of the "master teachers" in your building.

- Ask someone to observe the youngster at work and see if he or she notices anything you have not yet discovered about the child.

- Initiate special education procedures if you suspect the child truly has a learning problem.

- When you make accommodations to meet individual styles and rates of learning, exercise sensitivity. Make it the norm rather than the exception to have options and alternatives so that children do not feel singled out.

 Try This Today

Change the child's desk arrangement. Be sure he or she is seated among successful students who are also mature and caring. Then, provide some cooperative assignments and see whether you notice an improvement when the child is engaged in partner work with these peers.

How Do I Challenge Children
Who Learn Quickly and Easily?

- Be sure that some of your assignments are open ended so that children can rise to their highest level. For instance, instead of assigning a two-page report, simply assign a report.
- Include some free-choice reading time each day, and encourage the youngsters who are ready to do so to read challenging books.
- See if a colleague who teaches a higher grade would be willing to let some of your fast learners collaborate with some of his or her youngsters on a task, such as a science project or social studies investigation.
- Talk with the child's parents about how they can extend what you are doing in class into home learning.
- Be sure you notice and praise extra effort and quality products so that children feel appreciated for their talents.

 ### *Try This Today*

Make a photocopy of your class list. Keep it handy today and challenge yourself to notice and jot down a special talent or gift of each child in your class.

How Do I Accommodate the Varied
Interests of Children in My Classes?

- Find opportunities for children to select topics to study. For instance, they can choose the topic of a report on a famous person rather than being assigned a person.
- Be sure to include free-choice reading in your reading program.
- Ask children to relate information that they learn to their own experiences and knowledge. For instance, you can start projects by collecting and charting information about what children already know on the topic to be studied. You can also ask them to list questions that they would like to have answered. Their prior knowledge and current curiosity can help shape your instruction.
- Take advantage of opportunities to use children's special interests in the class. For instance, if a child has visited a country you are about to study,

the child and possibly other family members can be asked to present on the experience as part of your unit.

✔ ***Try This Today***

Create a simple inventory form for recording the children's and their families' hobbies, travel, and other interests. As a homework assignment, have children fill out the forms with their families. Use these surveys to spark ideas for unit themes and projects.

 For More Ideas and Information . . .

- Check out the "Teaching Diverse Learners" column in *Teaching K-8* magazine (1-800-678-8793).
- Read *All Children Are Special* by Greg Lang and Chris Berberich (Stenhouse, 1-800-988-9812).
- Talk to your building reading specialist or a district reading supervisor for additional techniques to support more leisurely learners and challenge avid learners.
- Take a look at *Too Scared to Learn* by Cara L. Garcia (Corwin Press, 1-805-499-9734).
- Read *How to Differentiate Instruction in Mixed-Ability Groups* by Carol Ann Tomlinson (Association for Supervision and Curriculum Development, 1-800-933-ASCD).
- Check out *Teaching Gifted Kids in the Regular Classroom* by Susan Winebrenner (Free Spirit).
- Skim *25 Terrific Literature Activities for Readers of All Learning Styles* by Lori Musso (Scholastic, 1-800-724-6527).
- Look for ideas in *I Can Learn!* by Gretchen Goodman (Stenhouse, 1-800-988-9812).
- Read *Educating Everybody's Children* by Robert W. Cole (Association for Supervision and Curriculum Development, 1-800-933-ASCD).
- Study *Learning Styles and Strategies* and *Teaching Styles and Strategies* by Harvey Silver et al. (Canter and Associates, 1-800-262-4347).

8

Questioning

Skillful questioning techniques are crucial tools for teachers. It is important to know not only what to ask but also when and how. Understanding how to handle the response is another key element in helping your children to learn and be at ease in your classroom.

What Kinds of Questions Should I Ask to Inspire Class Discussion?

- Ask questions that directly pertain to your lesson objective.
- Be sure your questions are challenging enough to be stimulating while not so hard that children cannot successfully respond.
- Limit the number of literal and recall questions you ask. Focus on high-level questions that will necessitate recall and application of details while motivating deeper thinking.
- As a matter of course, encourage children to defend their responses. Ask "Why do you think that?" and "How do you know?"
- Ask a few "meaty" questions rather than a lot of mundane ones.

 Try This Today

Integrate questions about process into your discussions. Ask "Where did you find that answer?" and "How did you figure out that solution?"

How Do I Get Lots of Children Involved in Class Discussion While Being Sure That Youngsters Feel Comfortable?

- When one child responds to a class discussion question, ask for a show of hands of those who agree. Then ask who disagrees. Ask a few dissenters to tell why they disagree.

- Give shy children a chance to "rehearse" responses by giving youngsters a few moments to discuss with a partner a question you have posed before sharing their answers with the whole class. This practice also gives everyone a chance to be involved rather than just the one on whom you call.

- Always give children the option of "passing" if they do not wish to share a response.

- Never call on a youngster to answer a question as a technique to refocus a child whom you suspect is not paying attention. Instead, simply say, "Pat, are you with us? I don't want you to miss anything."

- If you want to involve a child who has not volunteered a response, use an invitational tone such as, "I am interested in your ideas, too, Lee. Would you like to share a thought about this question?"

- Keep whole-class discussion to a minimum, because only one youngster can respond at a time. Also, incorporate partner and small-group discussion.

- Exercise wait time after asking a question. That is, slowly count to three to yourself before saying anything or calling on anyone. At first, it will seem like an interminable wait, but notice how many more children raise their hands to respond.

Try This Today

Give youngsters a minute to jot down a response on "thinking paper" (any piece of scrap paper) before you ask for whole-class sharing.

How Do I Inspire Children to Think at a High Level?

- Ask questions that start with "how" and "why" more than with "what," "where," and "when."

- Use a framework such as "Bloom's Taxonomy" or "Dimensions of Learning" to help you be aware of the kinds of questions and activities you assign.
- Teach children a simplified version of a thinking framework. From time to time, get a child to be a thinking observer and record the kinds of thinking used in class or a small group.
- Make up signs, symbols, or codes for different kinds of thinking. When you have children write in their journals in response to a reading selection, use the symbols in the margin to show children the kind of thinking they used. Hang up a poster of the symbols to make youngsters aware of the kinds of thinking they can do.

Try This Today

For one day, focus on asking questions for which you do not know the answer, such as "What would you have done in that situation?" and "What is your opinion about . . . ?" Note the effect that this has on the quality and interest of your discussions.

What Alternatives to Questions and Answers Can I Use to Encourage In-Depth Thinking?

- Make use of organizers so that children can graphically represent their ideas. Challenge children to create their own organizers after they become used to using the ones you furnish.

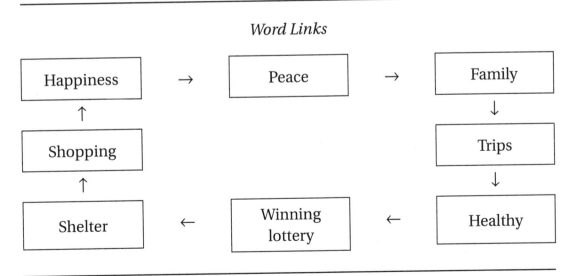

Word Links

Figure 8.1. Sample Child-Created Web

- Give children the assignment to act out concepts. For example, they can be asked to figure out a way to dramatize how to add fractions.
- Integrate concepts from two or more subject areas. For instance, children can be asked to write a poem about a historic event they are studying or to create a graph to show the different genres of literature they read during the year.

Try This Today

On scrap paper, jot down a few of the objectives you will be teaching over the next few days in a left-hand column. On the right, note how each of these skills is used in the world outside the classroom. Look back over the list to see if this information gives you an idea for a classroom simulation of a real-world use of skills.

For More Ideas and Information . . .

- Look at *101 Fresh and Fun Critical-Thinking Activities* by Laurie Rozakis (Scholastic, 1-800-724-6527).
- Read *Envisioning Process as Content* by Arthur L. Costa and Rosemarie M. Liebmann (Corwin Press, 1-805-499-9734).
- Look through *Multiple Intelligences in the Classroom* by Thomas Armstrong (Association for Supervision and Curriculum Development, 1-800-933-ASCD).
- Check out *Questioning Styles and Strategies* by Richard Strong et al. (Canter and Associates, 1-800-262-4347).
- See if you can find some new ideas in *Developing Minds* by Arthur Costa (Association for Supervision and Curriculum Development, 1-800-933-ASCD).

9

Assessing and Grading Progress

Measuring progress is an important part of a good classroom program. Assessing how the children are doing as you go along helps you to know when to slow down or speed up. Assessment covers a wide variety of techniques that go way beyond traditional tests and quizzes.

The companion piece to assessing is grading, or communicating progress to students and their families. Assigning grades can be tricky even for veteran teachers. Grading will be a lot less intimidating if you keep clearly focused on a sound philosophy and think through how you can use grades to support your learners.

What Kinds of Assessment Should I Use?

- You probably have no choice about some of the assessments you give. For instance, most districts use a type of norm-referenced test so that they can compare progress with other systems across the country. Some states and local districts also have exams that they have created and require to be administered. The best advice with these, especially if they do not exactly mesh with your philosophy, is to accept what you cannot change, as the axiom says.

- Supplement mandated assessments with your own formal and informal evaluations so that you can get information that is consistent with your program and specific to each child and unit.

- Remember that the purpose of assessment is to find out how each child is progressing on particular material so that you will know what he or she has learned and what has to be retaught.

- Make your test items and other assessment tasks as similar to your instruction as possible. For example, if children have been involved in discussing high-level questions in literature discussion groups as they read a novel, any assessment you do should also involve high-level questions about the novel.

- Realize that you do not always have to use a "testing event" to do classroom assessment. You can also assess progress by means such as looking at daily work, observing group work, and taking notes.

- Get children involved in self-evaluation often. Discuss with them the characteristics to be considered concerning successful completion of a particular task.

- Engage children in establishing their own goal contracts and then assessing their progress on achieving these.

Name _____	
Social Studies Unit on _____	
Date	Date
Goal	How did I do?
One thing I want to learn about in this unit is	I think I made A LITTLE, SOME, or LOTS OF progress. I know this because
One thing my teacher wants me to learn is	I think I made A LITTLE, SOME, or LOTS OF progress. I know this because
One thing I will do to be a successful social studies student is	I think I made A LITTLE, SOME, or LOTS OF progress. I know this because

Figure 9.1. Sample Goal Contract

✔ ***Try This Today***

Start a little notebook that contains a page for every child in your class. Keep the notebook with you, and make it a goal to write down a sign of progress you observe in each of three children that day.

How Do I Go About Establishing a Grading Policy?

- Check with your administrator or school handbook to see what the "givens" are about grading. Review this periodically so that you do not stray from district expectations and cause yourself problems with parents.
- Talk to other teachers about their grading philosophies. Then, make a "plus, minus, and explore" chart. Jot down what you like about what you have heard, what makes you uncomfortable, and what you need to think about and explore further.

TABLE 9.1. Grading Ideas

+	–	*Explore*
Giving children a chance to try again	Using extra credit unrelated to the original assignment	Find out what Pat does in third grade
Grading spelling separate from content	Posting grades on a class chart	

■ Make three columns on a sheet of paper. On the left, list skills or processes you need to teach. In the middle, list how you will assess or measure progress on each. In the right column, jot notes about how you will grade.

TABLE 9.2   Methods of Assessment

Skills/Processes	Method of Assessment	How to Grade
Multiplication tables	Fill-in quiz	Percentage correct
Comprehension— main idea	Journal entry on "What is the important idea in this article?"	Rubric

■ Offer children the option of redoing a particular assignment if they are unhappy with their grade on it. This can result in more learning, which is, of course, your goal.

■ Before you give an assignment, quiz, or test that you are going to grade, jot down a description of what each grade will look like (see Figure 9.2).

■ Remember that grades should indicate to what level a particular child has achieved specific teaching objectives. If you want to evaluate other characteristics, such as neatness, behavior, or participation, these should be reported separately.

■ When you offer extra credit as a means for improving grades, be sure that the task clearly and closely relates to the objective of the basic lesson and assignment.

Try This Today

Freewrite for several minutes about how you would handle grading if you had free rein to do whatever made sense to you. Reread your ideas to see what you can do or adapt and what you have to let go of based on school policy.

These standards can be used to assess and grade journal entries or other written responses to open-ended questions about a story that has been read. These standards can also be applied when you listen to the comments made in literature discussion groups. It is effective to share the standards with students before they read the material.

A response that deserves A TOP GRADE

_____ Shows the child understood complex aspects such as theme, mood, symbolism, and the author's message

_____ Connects elements of the story to the child's own life and experiences

_____ Comments on the author's style and effectiveness in relation to the development of the story

A response that deserves AN AVERAGE GRADE

_____ Shows the child understood the basic idea of the story and enough of the details to make sense of the plot

_____ Connects the elements of the story to the child's life in at least a surface manner

_____ Gives a reaction to his or her feelings about the story

A response that would deserve A LOW GRADE without further rereading and revision

_____ Shows a misunderstanding of the basic point of the story and/or confuses basic important details of the story

_____ Does not yet connect the story to his or her own life

_____ Does not yet react to the effectiveness of the story or feelings it inspires

These standards are appropriate for use with upper elementary and secondary schoolchildren.

Figure 9.2. Standards for Assignments Related to Reading of Stories
SOURCE: Joanne C. Strohmer and Clare Carhart, *Time-Saving Tips for Teachers* (1997, Corwin Press), p. 68.

How Do I Communicate
My Policy to Children?

- Talk to your class at the beginning of the year about how and why you give grades. Be sure to clarify in your own mind how you plan to use grades to support achievement and self-concept, not punish children. Communicate this commitment to the youngsters.
- Provide the standards for As, Bs, and so on in writing at the beginning of any major project or test. Encourage children to refer to these while they work so that they remember the requirements.

 Try This Today

Involve children in establishing the standards for grades on certain projects. Discuss with them what they think an "A" project or paper would look like, and so on. Do not worry that the children will be too easy on themselves; the opposite is usually true.

How Do I Communicate
My Policy to Parents?

- Go over your grading policy at your school's back-to-school night, orientation, or other first opportunity to meet with parents. Be sure that they understand how your grading system is designed to help, not punish, youngsters.
- Provide your grading policy in writing, and also explain it verbally to parents. Encourage them to keep these handouts for reference throughout the year and to refer to them when they discuss homework, tests, and other papers you send home with the children.
- Furnish examples of outstanding, satisfactory, and unsatisfactory work along with your grading policy so that parents get a clear picture. Point out the qualities that you associate with each grade a child can earn in your class.

Try This Today

Mark a folder "benchmark papers." Put it in an accessible place on your desk and start to save photocopies of satisfactory and exemplary papers related to the kind of assignment you often give. Later, you will be able to use these as a resource to show children and parents what you expect.

How Do I Use My Policy in Grading Assessments and Other Work?

- Mark items that were right to keep the focus on "can do's."
- Challenge yourself to find something to compliment about each paper you grade.
- When you are grading a large assignment like a piece of writing or a project, identify no more than three areas for improvement. More than this is overwhelming and can be counterproductive.
- Provide feedback privately. Graded papers should never be passed back by anyone but you, and grades should never be posted for others to see.
- Keep paper handy, and make a "to do" list for yourself about what you need to reteach and to whom as you grade papers.

Try This Today

Once in a while, before children hand in an assignment that you plan to grade, give them a moment to jot down the grade they think they should get. Have them write one sentence to explain why they think that grade is deserved.

How Can I Translate a Marking Period of Work Into a Report Card Grade?

- You can't! There is no way to boil down all the complexities of a child's work over time into a report card grade. Realize this and don't stress over it unduly.

- Make a plan at the beginning of the quarter or semester for how you are going to handle this challenging task so that you do not have to decide when you are up against a time crunch.
- Talk to colleagues about their approaches.
- Be sure you understand the school's and district's policies so that you do not cause yourself trouble. For instance, is the report card grade supposed to reflect an average, or where the child is at the end of the marking period?
- Talk with children about the report card grades as being just one indicator of their progress. Be sure you share other indicators with them.
- Use portfolios or other work samples you have collected as supplements to the report card so that you can share richer information with children and parents in addition to the report card grade.

 Try This Today

At best, report cards can be time consuming. At worst, they can be stressors because of philosophical clashes. Think ahead about scheduling your time during the days when you will be marking report cards. For example, arrange to have as few as possible other papers to grade. Also, think about putting some kind of relaxation or celebration on your calendar for the day after report cards are due.

What Do I Do When a Parent Questions a Grade I Have Given?

- Consider keeping portfolios of samples of each child's work so that you have something concrete to show parents to justify your grades.
- Listen to the parents' concerns without interrupting. Jot down key points you want to address when it is your turn to talk. Remember that grades can be an emotional issue for parents, so give them time to get their feelings out.
- Save copies of the standards and descriptions you prepared for grading the assignment or project in question so that you can show these to the parent and compare the child's work with the standards.
- In preparing for a conference with a parent who believes his or her child's grade was too low, make photocopies of papers that received better grades

than the child's. Cut off or black out the names and let the parent see these for a clearer picture of your expectations.

- Plan a few ideas concerning how you are going to help the child improve, and give concrete suggestions for supporting the growth at home.

- Let the concerned parent know about your policy related to letting children redo work if they are unsatisfied with their grades. Discuss how that policy can be used with the assignment in question.

Try This Today

For major assignments, send home with the graded assignment a copy of the rubrics or standards you used to grade. This will help some parents be more specific in communicating the area of their concern.

For More Ideas and Information . . .

- Read *Challenging the Mind, Touching the Heart: Best Assessment Practices* by Robert A. Reineke (Corwin Press, 1-805-499-9734).

- Study *Portfolio Assessment: Getting Started Grades K-8* (Scholastic, 1-800-724-6527).

- Look at *Communicating Student Learning* by Tom Guskey (Association for Supervision and Curriculum Development, 1-800-933-ASCD).

- Get a copy of *Assessment* by Lois Bridges (Stenhouse, 1-800-988-9812).

- Check out *Quick Tips—Writing Effective Report Card Comments* by Susan Shafer (Scholastic, 1-800-724-6527).

- Examine *Expanding Student Assessment* by Vito Perrone (Association for Supervision and Curriculum Development, 1-800-933-ASCD).

- Read *Well-Chosen Words* by Brenda Miller Power and Kelly Chandler (Stenhouse, 1-800-988-9812).

10
Assigning Homework

Homework provides you with a great way to connect with families and extend your program into your children's homes. You can make the most of this opportunity by assigning high-quality homework tasks.

How Can I Make Homework Worthwhile?

- Use homework to provide meaningful practice of objectives you taught in class.

- Be sure youngsters understand what they are supposed to do and can do it independently. Homework is not for teaching new skills. Ask children to paraphrase back to you what you are asking them to do. Provide modeling by doing one item in class.

- Focus on homework that helps build good habits, such as reading for a specified time each evening.

- Homework can be used to assess prior knowledge in preparation for new learning. For instance, children could be asked to jot down five things they already know about early colonies as homework the day before starting a new unit on the topic.

- Youngsters can be asked to apply something they have learned in class as a homework assignment. For example, after teaching how to punctuate quotations, youngsters could be asked to write five quotes from their families that evening.

- Do not feel compelled to assign daily homework unless this is a school requirement. Only assign homework when there is a valid reason to do so.
- Be cautious about assigning children to complete unfinished classwork at home. Children may be having trouble finishing work because they do not yet understand the concepts well. In those cases, it would not make sense to assign them to complete the work independently.
- Use homework assignments as a way to gather materials or information for classwork. For instance, children could be asked to interview family members to find out their favorite books in order to prepare a program or bulletin board for library week or book month.

Try This Today

Do not "overassign" homework. If five mathematics problems will show you which of the children understand and which need more help, why assign 20 problems?

How Do I Encourage Children to Complete Their Homework?

- Provide alternatives to standard paper-and-pencil tasks for homework. Sometimes, children can draw, create simple models, or read articles instead of doing worksheets or textbook assignments.
- Make homework enjoyable by adding cute drawings to a worksheet or by including a fun part like a quick puzzle or joke.
- Involve families in the homework. Have children ask parents to write a little response on the bottom of their homework. For instance, you could have a line that invites a family member to jot down a comment about one thing the child did well on the assignment.

Try This Today

Let children make some choices about homework tasks from time to time. You could ask them to select 3 out of 10 science questions, for example.

How Do I Ensure That Children, Not Parents, Complete Homework?

- Send home a note at the beginning of school explaining the benefits to the child of completing homework. Spell out a few examples of the kind of family input that is helpful to the child's learning. For instance, you might suggest that instead of spelling words for the child, the parent help him or her make a little word wall or chart of commonly used words to keep in the place where homework is done.

- Keep the tone of homework light and nonthreatening. Be sure that children and parents realize that you assign homework to give children extra practice and to give yourself a way to determine which skills are learned and which need to be retaught. If homework is not a high-stakes event, parents may not feel compelled to participate in getting it perfect.

- Include a box on the homework paper for the parent to fill in indicating how independently the child was able to complete the work.

(Add to the bottom of homework worksheet)

On this homework assignment, I helped   Stevie _____

a lot   (a little)   not at all

Comments:

Parent: Mrs. White _____

Figure 10.1. Homework Help Chart

Try This Today

Include an optional parent involvement part in some assignments. For example, after the child has completed an assignment telling ways in which the early American lifestyle differed from that of today, parents could be invited to add another way that they know about in a special box at the end of the worksheet or paper.

How Do I Handle Grading Homework?

- Do a quick check of homework while youngsters are doing a warm-up assignment. Make up a homework checklist, and mark it as you circulate.

- Involve children in self-checking homework as often as possible. This practice gives them instant feedback and prevents you from going home with a pile of papers.

- Spot check at least some homework. By checking a few answers on a worksheet at the beginning of class, for example, you can get an idea of how children are progressing without taking up too much class time.

- Let parents know how and why you will grade homework so that their expectations will be realistic.

 Try This Today

Do big-picture grading of some homework. That is, designate the work exemplary, satisfactory, or in need of more practice instead of analyzing every detail. Remember that the point is to get a general idea whether you need to reteach or move on. You don't always need to agonize over details.

What Do I Do When Children Do Not Bring in Their Homework?

- Ask the child if he or she can identify the reason for the problem. Try to determine if it relates to difficulty level, motivation, or a home factor. See if you can cook up a solution together.

- If some children forget to do their assignments, consider asking all children to keep assignment books. Provide time at the end of each subject for them to record their homework assignment.

- Have children keep personal charts that they use to mark off completion of homework each day that it is assigned.

Homework Check-Up

Check your homework and then check the following items:

Did I follow the directions exactly?   _____

Did I understand what I was doing?   _____

Is my work neat and easy to read?   _____

How long did it take me to do the work?   _____

Figure 10.2. Homework Self-Check

- Create a class incentive program. Award points for each homework assignment completed. Provide a celebration when a specified number of points are earned by the class.
- Do not hesitate to call parents to check on reasons why homework has not been completed. Family support may solve the problem.

Try This Today

Get children to pair up with homework buddies who will exchange phone numbers and call each other to check assignments and clear up any confusion.

For More Ideas and Information . . .

- Read *Help! It's Homework Time* by Lee Canter and Marlene Canter (Lee Canter and Associates, 1-800-262-4347).
- Also check out *Teaching Responsible Homework Habits* (Canter and Associates, 1-800-262-4347).

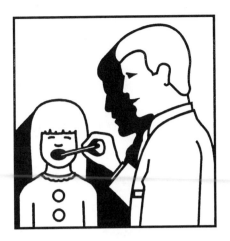

11

Catching up Absentees

You cannot avoid the fact that youngsters will be out of the classroom from time to time for illness or family situations. Plan ahead to use effective, efficient routines so that you can help these youngsters catch up on what they have missed.

How Do I Help Children Who Have Been Out Sick to Catch Up?

■ When you take role each morning, invite someone to be a Catch-Up Buddy for each of the absent youngsters. You can hand out a little checklist of the responsibilities of a Catch-Up Buddy (see Figure 11.1).

Catch-Up Buddy Checklist

Dear *Jackie* ,

Thank you for agreeing to be *Melissa's* Catch-Up Buddy while he or
she is absent. Your jobs will be to:

_____ Get an extra copy to give to your buddy of any handouts I give out.

_____ Meet with your buddy before class starts the first day back to tell
what we did.

_____ Tell your buddy about homework.

It would be great if you could make a phone call to see how your buddy is
doing and tell about what happened at school, but it is okay if you can't.

Thanks for your help.

Mr. Smith

Figure 11.1. Catch-Up Buddy Checklist

- If your school has an automated phone message system for homework,
  provide sufficient information so that children can catch up on at least
  some work. Ask parents early in the year to check the message when their
  children are absent.
- Use time such as group work time or silent reading time on the day when
  an absentee comes back to brief him or her on catch-up work.
- If you have any older children who are tutors or any parent volunteers, consider making it one of their routine tasks to help returning absentees go
  through their folders of catch-up work.

Try This Today

Designate a container that will hold a few file folders as an absentee
catch-up box. Whenever you pass out worksheets or other handouts, put extras in the files for anyone who is absent that day.

What Do I Do When Parents Ask for Work Because They Want to Take Their Child on a Trip?

- At your first meeting with parents, stress the importance of having children in school as often as possible. Let them know that there are certain things youngsters cannot make up, such as group discussions, to illustrate the seriousness of having youngsters out when they do not have to be.

- Recognize the reality that children will be out at certain times of the year. For instance, in some districts, parents often extend certain vacation times or take time off if other members of the family are on holiday. Plan worthwhile activities during those times, but consider the practicality of reviews and/or enrichment activities if you expect major absences.

- Consider preparing some "standard" reading, writing, and other assignments that you can have handy in a packet for traveling families. The activities may be different from those you will do in class, but they will still provide worthwhile learning while the child is away. They can help take the stress out of trying to duplicate in directions and handouts what will happen in class.

Try This Today

Be on the lookout for commercially prepared materials that address skills that you teach. Put them in a folder and save them for occasions when parents ask for work. Although these resources might not be the ones you choose to use in your classroom, they may still provide worthwhile practice that a parent can implement so that you don't have to try to create lesson plans "to go."

For More Ideas and Information . . .

- Find ready-to-use activities that you might be able to give parents in *The Best of the Good Apple Newspaper.*

- Use your teacher's edition of textbooks as a source of ideas that you did not use with your class but that you could give to a parent for travel use.

12

Handling the Paperwork

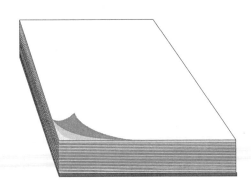

When you went into the field of teaching, you did so because you wanted to work with children. You have also found out, however, that teaching involves a lot of paperwork. As in any other profession, effective techniques will help you handle this part of the job.

How Do I Handle Grading Papers?

- Grade for a few skills at a time. Do not mark everything on a paper.
- Have children write the objective for the lesson on the top of a worksheet, or you can include it on the master before you run it off. Let parents know that sometimes you will just be grading the acquisition of the objective listed at the top of the page.
- Avoid assigning huge lists of problems or questions. Children can get adequate practice from doing a few examples. This approach lessens your paper load while giving you feedback about whether or not you need to reteach and assign a few more practice tasks.
- Use peer checking frequently. Not only does this technique provide an alternative to your having to grade everything, but it is beneficial to the checkers. Build in an accountability component so that checkers remember that they need to take this responsibility seriously. For instance, you could have a small box at the bottom of worksheets where checkers can sign their names and give one compliment and suggest one area for more practice.

- Get a rubber stamp that says "Draft" or "Unchecked" to alert parents and others to the fact that some papers they see might not be fully checked and graded.
- Let children self-check work. If you use this practice, frequently remind the children that grading is to help them see what they know and what they still need to learn. Reinforce the fact that they can redo work if they have lots of errors. These assurances should help children be honest about evaluating their work.

Try This Today

Make up a self-report slip for children to use when you have them mark their own papers. This idea will help make self-checking a worthwhile activity so that you do not have to personally check each paper yourself.

Name: *Maryanne*

Things that I can congratulate myself on:

I got 8 out of 10 right.

My work was neat.

I did better than last time.

Things I am going to fix:

Correct #4 and #5

Fix the spelling in #6

The grade I think I should get is *B* because

I didn't get them all right but I came close and I know how to fix my mistakes.

Figure 12.1. Self-Report on Self-Checking

How Do I Keep Up With Responding to Journals?

- Stagger due dates so that you do not have to respond to all of the journals on the same evening. For instance, different reading groups, different parts of the alphabet, or different rows could be due on different days of the week.

- Have alternative ways of responding so that they get used to you not always providing lengthy answers to their entries. For instance, sometimes you can use a sticker and a short-word response. Mix it up so that they never know what to expect.

- Train children to respond to each other's entries from time to time. The training should include mini-lessons that provide examples of good responses, ideas about being sensitive to the writer, and guidelines about staying on topic.

- Occasionally, ask parents to write responses to their child's journals.

 Try This Today

Find some little bits of time, such as when children are reading or completing assignments, to pull children one by one. Skim their most recent journal entry and talk to them for just a moment about their entry. For instance, you might want to give them one compliment and ask one question. Journal responses do not always have to be written.

How Do I Manage All the Mail I Get From Other People in the Building and From the Central Office?

- Stop by your mailbox at a specific time every day, such as at the end of the day or when you have just dropped children off for lunch. If you discipline yourself to do this regularly, the quantity of mail will not build up.

- Consider the idea of taking your mail and a pen with you when you are on duty in a time-out room, or when you have to attend a meeting that may not require your full attention all the time. Sort the mail into piles, such as things to throw out before you leave the room, items you can handle quickly by jotting an immediate response on the bottom, and items that will take a little more time.
- Be ruthless about discarding junk mail. Keep only those ads and announcements you will actually use.
- Train a responsible child to sort the mail from the promotional pieces.

Try This Today

Put the day's mail in an envelope or folder and carry it with you. See what little slices of time you can find to deal with it as you go through your day.

How Do I Store Important Papers?

- Avoid loose papers like the plague! Have clearly marked folders, notebooks, and manila envelopes for any papers you need to be able to find again.
- Sort folders of important papers into file cabinets or bins. For example, have one drawer or box for teaching ideas, one for parent form letters, and so on. Arrange the folders within each bin alphabetically.
- Store important papers that you need frequently in cabinets or boxes near where you use them. Purposely put important papers you do not need to access frequently or quickly in containers away from your main work areas.
- Try to avoid storing some important school papers at school and others at home. If you store them all in one place, you will not get confused about what is where.

Try This Today

Get a package of self-adhesive labels. Keep these on hand with a nice marker so that you can make labels that are clear and pleasing to your eye.

How Do I Help Children Organize and Store Their Papers?

- Decide before school opens what kinds of papers children may need to store and determine the kind of storage you wish them to use. Let parents know as soon as possible what their youngsters will need.

- Jot down a little chart on a piece of scrap paper. This may help you organize your thoughts about how children can organize.

TABLE 12.1   Storage of Children's Work

Kinds of work	How to organize/store
Writing in progress	Alpha-order folders in bins on windowsill
Social studies notes	In three-ring binder with unit dividers
Science mini-labs	In spiral notebook on shelves near science centers

- Take a few moments here and there to provide mini-lessons on how to organize notebooks and portfolios, and other ways to store important papers. Children are not born with this skill. They need some instruction.

- Check youngsters' notebooks or portfolios frequently so that you can help them get back on track if they are having trouble organizing. You could simply ask them to put the materials on their desks so that you can take a quick look while they are involved in some other activity.

- Occasionally, award little prizes or notes of appreciation when you see someone doing a good job of keeping materials organized.

- Provide storage bins or decorated boxes for children's folders when possible so that these materials are less likely to get lost or messed up from being jammed in desks.

 Try This Today

Be on the lookout for youngsters who have a knack for organization. Show their notebooks, portfolios, or other materials. Comment on why they are effective and how they are organized. Better yet, ask the owner to share his or her strategies for keeping organized.

For More Ideas and Information . . .

- Read *Time-Saving Tips for Teachers* by Joanne C. Strohmer and Clare Carhart (Corwin Press, 1-805-499-9734).

- Look at *File Don't Pile* by Pat Doff (St. Martin's Press).

- See what ideas you can find in *The Office Clutter Cure* by Don Aslett (Betterway Books, 1-800-289-0963).

- Check out *Organize Your Workplace* by Odette Pollar (Crisp Publications, 1-800-462-6420).

13

Planning for Substitutes

The nature of teaching is that you not only must plan well when working with children, but it is also necessary to plan ahead for those times when you are not able to be with your class. Providing carefully constructed substitute plans will ensure that your children have a beneficial learning experience even when you have to be out of the building.

How Do I Prepare for Having a Substitute When I Plan to Be Out of the Building?

- Try to plan review lessons of what you have taught on the preceding days rather than asking the substitute to introduce new concepts.
- Be as clear as possible in writing out directions. Leave key items such as seating charts on your desk.
- See if you and another teacher can work out a collaborative relationship. That is, ask if you may quickly go over your substitute plans with this colleague so that she or he can answer questions for the substitute. Offer to reciprocate by doing the same for your colleague when he or she plans to be out.
- Cultivate a good relationship with a substitute who does a particularly nice job for you. Show appreciation of his or her conscientiousness by sending a note or making a point of calling to express your appreciation. Request this substitute whenever possible.

- Plan self- or peer-checking components of lessons so that you do not come back to a pile of papers to grade.

- Do not be afraid to express your concern if serving on a committee or taking part in a training effort would cause undue stress and unduly interrupt your children's program. In some cases, the person asking you to attend may appreciate your input and be able to accommodate your need to stay in school or arrange an alternative plan.

Try This Today

Ask your children what they think a substitute teacher would need to know about the class and classroom. Take notes about any ideas they have that are helpful.

How Do I Handle Providing Plans When I Need to Be Away From School Unexpectedly?

- Use a little bit of your summer vacation to plan a few review and extension lessons that could be used at any time of the year. Place these in a clearly marked notebook or folder that you leave on your desk at all times. The time you spend during the relatively less hectic days of July or August to do this will pay off in peace of mind when you need plans to get you through a bout of flu in February.

- Rely on worthwhile commercial materials to help with emergency plans for a substitute. Buy books of some reproducible sheets that could be used by your children to reinforce skills you have already presented or to address a skill you would like them to learn but probably will not have time to cover. Tear out selected exercises with directions for how you wish these to be used and put them in a substitute folder.

- Keep an up-to-date seating chart in your substitute folder or notebook.

Try This Today

Ask a colleague at your grade level if she or he has any activities that are good to leave for substitute teachers. Offer to share some of your activities.

How Do I Inspire Youngsters to Behave for a Substitute?

- Consider using the term "guest teacher" instead of substitute to call attention to the fact that this person should be treated with consideration.

- Teach some mini-lessons on how children should work with a substitute teacher. Ask them to collaborate with you to generate a chart of productive and cooperative behaviors to keep in mind when you are not there. Hang the chart, and go over these behaviors near the end of the day before a substitute will be in your room.

- On the day before you plan to be out, also put up a chart that is headed "Compliments From Our Guest Teacher." Explain to the children that you will be asking the substitute to jot down some examples of mature behavior that he or she notices. Leave a note for the substitute requesting that this be done in order to provide positive reinforcement.

- Sometimes, you may want to provide a little treat or celebration in recognition of good reports from the substitute.

- Early in the year, engage children in a conversation about what it must feel like to be a substitute teacher coming into a new class for the first time. Help them brainstorm ways to be welcoming and helpful to a guest teacher. Remind them of their ideas whenever you know you will be out of class.

- Ask one of your colleagues with whom you have a collaborative relationship to get into the habit of stopping by your class occasionally when you are out and very obviously asking the substitute how the children are doing and what kind of report he or she would like your colleague to give you when you return. Of course, you would reciprocate by doing the same for this coworker when he or she has a substitute.

✓ *Try This Today*

Play a game with your children. Engage them in pretending you are a substitute for the day. Make up a new name for yourself and perhaps dress differently than you usually do. Introduce yourself and tell something about your fictitious character. Use this situation as a vehicle for pointing out how they are expected to act with a substitute. For example, you might pretend you do not know the routine for taking the class to the cafeteria and have the youngsters help you.

How Do I Handle the "Aftermath" of Being Out of the Building?

- Plan lessons that involve reviewing and updating from the day before. The first day you are back is not a good time to launch into a new unit if you can avoid it.
- Get to school a little early so that you can check your desk and see what communications and work the substitute has left for you.
- Remember to reinforce good behavior that children demonstrated.
- Deal with any reports of problematic behavior with those individuals directly. Talk to the children about your expectations. Also, do not hesitate to call parents and enlist their support in improving behavior.

Try This Today

If unchecked papers have been left for you, hand them back to the children and use self- or peer checking to provide feedback without having a double load of work your first evening after being out. This technique will also help you and the children review what was done the day before so that you can gauge what needs to be done next.

For More Ideas and Information . . .

- Choose a substitute whom you admire. Ask him or her to tell you three things that teachers do that are helpful and three things that he or she wishes teachers would do differently.
- Look at the substitute's situation from his or her perspective by reviewing *Substitute Teaching* by Barbara Pronin (St. Martin's Griffin, 175 Fifth Avenue, New York, NY, 10010).
- Check out *A Sourcebook for Substitute Teachers and Others* by Miriam Freedman and Teri Peel (Addison-Wesley).

14 Using Volunteers

Parent and community volunteers can be a bonus to your program. They can help you provide experiences for the children that you might not be able to accomplish on your own. Volunteers can also handle some of the routine aspects of your program so that you have more quality time with your youngsters.

What Kinds of Jobs Should I Give to Volunteers?

- Create a simple survey form to find out about the special talents and interests of your volunteers or potential volunteers. If people are doing what they like, they do it better and more reliably.

- Give volunteers jobs that have the most positive impact on students. In some cases, that may mean having them work directly with youngsters. In many instances, however, it will mean doing clerical, artistic, or organizational tasks so that you have more time with the children.

- Find volunteers who are artistic and give them opportunities to do bulletin boards, decorations, posters, and charts. Also, see if your volunteers with an artistic flair are willing to prepare materials for arts and crafts projects and, perhaps, be on hand to help youngsters when they use the materials.

- Consider how volunteers can provide the one-on-one attention you are not always able to furnish. These activities might include reading to a child, listening to a child read, and giving a child feedback on something he or she has written. Volunteers can also help as math, science, and social studies tutors.

- Identify a parent who can help with secretarial and communications tasks, such as making some of your phone calls and writing notes.

- Seek out computer-literate volunteers who can do Web searches or other computer work for you.

- Also, invite technology-buff parents to be on hand when your youngsters are using computers so that they can provide additional assistance when youngsters have questions or run into problems.

- Be cautious about giving volunteers jobs that require your specialized expertise. For instance, it is risky to ask parents to conduct revision conferences with children's writing unless you have trained them in issues such as looking at ideas as well as mechanics, respecting author rights, and showing sensitivity in how they phrase suggestions.

Try This Today

Think of one or two aspects of your job that you do not like. Brainstorm how a parent volunteer could help with those tasks. For instance, you might hate correcting math problems. Believe it or not, there is a parent in your school community who thinks it is relaxing to sit down with a pile of papers to grade once in a while.

How Can I Plan for Volunteers?

- Plan ahead. Do not stress yourself by waiting until a parent shows up to decide how he or she can help you and the children.

- During summer break or some other time when you have extra time, brainstorm generic kinds of jobs you might want volunteers to do, and make up a direction card or folder for each task that will be ready in advance.

- Create a chart of tasks that need to be done. Store or hang it in a place that will be accessible to volunteers who come into your room. Direct them to a task on the chart or ask them to choose one.

Date	Jobs	Completed?	Comments
3/7	Listen to Lee read Put up new chart	✔ ✔	Work on expression
3/8	Check math Help Maria	 ✔	Half done She's got it!

Figure 14.1. Sample Chart of Volunteer Jobs

- Think in terms of scheduling people by expertise. Have a brief meeting with your potential volunteers. Find out which area of expertise each has: art, former teacher, computers, secretarial, and so on. Channel relevant tasks to each and let them schedule the time to do these.

- Always have a back-up plan in mind in case a volunteer does not appear when expected.

Try This Today

Keep a notebook on your desk that you can use to jot down particular children's names and what kind of one-on-one help each could use as you notice these situations. Then, you will have a list of ideas the next time a volunteer is scheduled to be in your room.

What Should I Do When a Volunteer Is Not Working Out?

- Formulate a sensitive way of telling the parent how you need him or her to do the job instead of criticizing the way it is being done. For example, you could say, "Mr. Jones, it is such a help to me when you meet with children about their writing. They get so much more individual attention. As a matter of fact, it is going so well that I think you could go to the next step of talking with them about more than their spelling and address one of the things on this list that I will give you as a reference."

- Notice what additional skills or interests the volunteer might have. See if you can channel interest in that direction instead of continuing with the job he or she might not be suited to do. For example, "Ms. Smith, you have been working with that small group for a couple of times, and I notice that they haven't been on task for you. I also noticed that they loved the drawing you did when you met with them today. Would you be willing to use your artistic skills to help with our bulletin boards?"

 Try This Today

Use an approach designed to prevent problems when you first talk to someone about volunteering in your classroom. Use wording such as, "I have an idea I want to try. Let's have you work with Johnny's group for a day or two. Then, I might change what I need you to do." This gives you a graceful out if the task you have assigned is not matching the volunteer's strengths.

How Do I Show Appreciation for Volunteers and Keep Them From Burning Out?

- The day after a good experience with a volunteer, have your children, or at least a few representatives, write thank-you letters or draw pictures to send to the volunteer.

- If you have a particularly effective volunteer on whom you call regularly, challenge your children to write picture books starring this volunteer as a special guest teacher in your classroom. Primary grade children could collaborate with you on a group-written big book.

- Have a volunteer appreciation day occasionally.

- Invite a favorite volunteer to special programs or parties with your class. This will not only show appreciation but also help the children become more familiar with the person.

Try This Today

Stop at a store and get some note cards. Keep these on your desk so that they will be handy for you to take a moment to write a thank-you note when you have had a good experience with a volunteer.

For More Ideas and Information . . .

- Find out if your state or local government has a volunteer program. Request literature on working with volunteers.
- Get *Easy to Manage Reading and Writing Conferences* by Laura Robb (Scholastic, 1-800-724-6527).

15

Managing Field Trips

Often, field trip memories are among some of the most enjoyable and vivid for youngsters as they look back on their elementary education. Field trips can be positive memories for you, too, if you call upon your planning and organizational skills. In addition to being memorable, school field trips must be educational. High-quality preparatory and follow-up activities will help your children get the most out of these experiences.

How Do I Decide Where to Take Children on Field Trips to Ensure That They Have Worthwhile Experiences?

- Tie field trips directly into some part of your curriculum. If children see the connection between the excursion and what they are learning, they will be more likely to get something out of it and also to behave with their school manners rather than their playing-in-the-neighborhood behaviors.

- Be on the lookout for simple, local sites that enrich your program. Not every field trip has to be an extravaganza.

- When you are attending workshops and other networking opportunities, ask what worthwhile locations your colleagues have found.

- Send out a survey to parents of your youngsters. Mention a few upcoming units and ask them if they know of sites to visit. Some may be able to have children visit their offices, businesses, or plants. Others may know of some interesting locations as a result of family outings.

Try This Today

Look in the "local" section of your neighborhood bookstore for paperbacks on day trips in the area. You could get some able readers from your own class or an upper grade to review the books to find locations related to a specific unit you plan to teach. Not only does this cut down on your work, but it provides the youngsters with an authentic research opportunity.

How Do I Plan for Field Trips?

- First of all, see if you can find a parent volunteer who would like to coordinate the excursion or at least do some portions of the work.

- If there is any possible way, try to visit the site first yourself to be sure it is appropriate and so that you can get ideas about how to prepare the children and how to follow up the experience. If you cannot visit, call and ask lots and lots of questions about aspects of the trip.

- Encourage one or more other teachers who teach the unit related to the field trip to collaborate with you. Make a "to do" list and divide the work.

Try This Today

Get children involved. Early in the process, ask them to brainstorm what needs to be done to make the trip a success. Assign some parts to youngsters. For instance, if they are intermediate grade children, they can write or e-mail for information, make name tags, and write to their parents about the trip.

How Do I Handle Parent Volunteers on Field Trips?

- Consider having a brief, pre-trip orientation meeting at some point before the scheduled event. This seems like extra work, but it can pay off in a smoother experience.

- Write out a sheet for parents who will chaperone a trip. Include any vital information about the site as well as expectations for behavior that you have conveyed to the children. (File the sheet after the trip if you think you will visit the site again another year.)

- When you solicit volunteers to accompany your class on the trip, gently but clearly lay out what you need from them in terms of managing the group of children you will assign them to supervise. Diplomatically let them know that you will need to depend on them to do certain tasks.

- At the end of each field trip, jot yourself notes about what worked relative to volunteers and on what you could improve. Keep these notes in your field trip folder or notebook to help you remember what the experience has taught you.

✓ *Try This Today*

Jot down notes about how your "dream chaperone" would operate. Now, look back over your notes and pick one or two elements of the dream that you might be able to make come true or nearly true. Get to work on implementing them.

How Do I Encourage Appropriate Behavior on Field Trips?

- If you have been to the site before (and that is an important step if at all possible), think ahead about the possible temptations and pitfalls. For instance, maybe you are taking them to a museum where there are certain displays that are not to be touched. If you know these considerations ahead of time, you can alert the children to your expectations.

- Be sure that children have something worthwhile to do on the trip that is related to your curriculum unit. For instance, they might be assigned a checklist of things to find at a historic site you are visiting. Or they might have brainstormed questions that they are to try to answer on the trip.

- Conduct a few mini-lessons on travel behavior. Address aspects such as riding on the bus, cooperating with parent volunteers, listening to and interacting with tour guides, and dealing with their peers.

- Engage children in writing a language experience story with you about visiting the site. Encourage them to incorporate details about how they will act in various situations during the trip.

Try This Today

Several days before the event, have children brainstorm a list of good travel manners. Put these on a chart and review them each day before the field trip.

What Do I Do as a Follow-Up for a Field Trip?

- Have children return to their list of questions or checklist of information on which they were asked to focus during the trip. Discuss what they found and what they still want to know. Help them figure out how they can fill in gaps in information.
- Shortly after the field trip, ask each youngster to identify three things that he or she learned that are most important. Create a class list of some of these ideas and hang it on the wall to keep the information fresh in children's minds.
- Have youngsters translate what they learned into another form. For instance, they could create a picture book for a preschooler about what they learned. This activity could be done as a language experience big book if you teach a primary grade.

Try This Today

To be sure that children are retaining their learning over time, ask youngsters to recall the previous field trip you took with them, even if it was some time ago. Have them recall what they learned. This can be done in a discussion, drawing, or short journal entry. If the trip was important enough to schedule, it is important that children maintain the benefits of the experience past the day after the trip.

For More Ideas and Information . . .

- Find out if a parent in your school community is a travel agent. Ask him or her for tips that would help with class trips.

- Contact your local office of tourism. Ask for a packet of information about sites of interest. See which sites relate to your instructional units. As an alternative, talk to the tourism representative about your units and see what he or she can suggest.

- Check out *The World's Best Travel Games* by Sheila Anne Barry (Sterling Publications, 387 Park Avenue South, New York, NY 10016).

16
Handling Classroom Parties, Plays, and Special Events

Special events are an important part of a well-balanced elementary program. These occasions can be a challenge for the teacher who is coordinating them. With careful decision making and help from volunteers, you can enjoy these times with your children.

How Can I Provide Children With Celebrations and Stay Sane?

- Think small and simple.
- Elicit assistance from as many helpful parent volunteers as possible.
- Keep the events short and as close to the end of the day as feasible. Youngsters do not have to have a party that lasts a long time in order to feel they have celebrated.
- To keep the actual party short without seeming like Scrooge, extend the theme into the day's learning. For instance, if your class celebrates Valentine's Day, you can put hearts on math worksheets, assign language arts writing and reading on the topic of friendship, and so on. You can honor the holiday within the context of the workday.
- Try to have children out of the room just before the party so you can set up. For instance, things run smoother if you put a snack on each desk rather than make it necessary for children to get up and serve themselves. This

can be accomplished by planning the party after the youngsters are out for a special subject or by seeing if someone can take the youngsters outside for a short break. If that is impossible, parent volunteers could set up while you take the children to the media center or at least to a corner of your room and read a holiday story to them.

What Are Some Tips for Making Guest Speaker Occasions Run Smoothly?

- Be sure your guest speaker's topic is closely related to your curriculum.
- If at all possible, be sure you have heard the speaker or gotten an endorsement from someone whose judgment you trust.
- It often works best to have a guest speaker at the end of or at least well into the unit of study rather than at the beginning. This approach ensures that children will know something about the topic, attend well, and have relevant questions and comments.
- Help children identify questions they might ask that would add to their knowledge. List these and then discuss which might be the most appropriate.

 Try This Today

Help children brainstorm the kind of behaviors that will make a guest feel welcome. Put these on chart paper and review them for a few days before the event.

How Do I Handle Assemblies?

- Explicitly discuss audience behaviors that are appropriate in a large group setting. Help children envision how difficult it is to talk or perform before a large group and how important their consideration is.
- Prevent problems by separating children who may provide temptations for each other. Do this in a positive vein by telling these individuals privately that you have noticed it can be harder to attend when they are with a certain buddy. Assure the child that you want everything to go well, so you are going to ask the two friends not to sit together this time.
- Brief the children about the topic of the assembly before the presentation.

- Provide a quiet activity before the assembly such as reading aloud to the youngsters, if possible.

- Give the children a purpose for listening to the assembly presentation. Plan at least a brief follow-up activity, and tell them what they need to listen for during the event to be ready to do the follow-up when they return.

- Be sure that the children know the behaviors you will be looking for during the assembly. Take a piece of paper and a pen with you so that you can jot down compliments to share when everyone returns to the classroom.

- Have children self-evaluate their audience behavior after a presentation. Ask them to be explicit about what was commendable and what goals they need to set for next time.

Try This Today

Put the words "Audience Applause" on a chart. Hang it on a wall and ask children to brainstorm three audience behaviors they believe are the most important. Record these on the chart and refer to them any time children are preparing to go to an assembly.

How Can I Include Student Plays, Videos, and Other Performances in My Program?

- Keep projects that involve dramatic presentations simple. You don't want to gobble up lots of class time with major productions involving complicated costuming, scripting, and settings.

- Remember that some children may be very uncomfortable with dramatic presentations. Let them use an alternative method of participating. Forcing a shy youngster to perform will do more harm than good.

- Not everyone has to be involved in one big extravaganza presentation. Consider having several small, simple opportunities so that everyone who wishes to can participate some time during the year.

- Find out if there is a parent in your community who is interested in drama. Invite him or her to be your consultant.

- If you have a high school in your neighborhood, see if students from the drama program might want to collaborate with your youngsters on a play or video project.

✔ ***Try This Today***

Ask your media specialist to find some books of simple plays for your class.

 For More Ideas and Information . . .

- Look at *Homespun Fun* (St. Martin's Press).
- See what you can find in *Plays Around the Year* (Scholastic, 1-800-724-6527).
- Look for ideas in *Terrific Parties for Kids* by Janice Hubbard Holmes (Horizon Publications, P.O. Box 490, Bountiful, UT 84011-0490.
- See what you can find in *The Incredible Indoors Game Book* by Bob Gregson (Fearon Teaching Aids, 23740 Hawthorne Boulevard, Torrance, CA 90505).

17

Making Parent Contacts Productive

Parents are not only their children's first teachers, but they are also their continuous teachers and education coordinators throughout their youngsters' school careers. The key to positive parent-teacher contacts is remembering that parents want success for their children just as you do. What you may sometimes have to discuss is a way of achieving that success that both you and the parents can support.

When Do I Need to Contact Parents?

- You need to contact parents as soon as you are feeling a concern either about academic progress or behavior. It is easier to talk about a tiny problem that has just started than a huge one that has been allowed to fester.

- Just as important, parent contact needs to be made to congratulate youngsters for good efforts and progress. It is a great idea to set the goal for yourself of writing at least three positive notes or making three calls to pay compliments to children each week. The little time you take to do this will pay off in parent support and child enthusiasm.

- Contact parents when they can help you with their expertise. Ask for their advice about their child, or invite them to share a special skill or experience with your class.

- Connect with parents to let them know what you are doing with your program. A half-hour spent in putting together a one-page newsletter telling of upcoming attractions will help parents feel "in the know" and also give them a chance to volunteer their services or materials related to specific projects and units.

■ As often as possible, invite parents to be part of your program by coming to parties, reading books that the children are reading and joining discussion groups, and being part of the audience when projects and presentations are shared.

Try This Today

Think of a parent you have not talked to recently. Give him or her a quick call, or send a little note telling one thing you appreciate about the child.

How Should I Set Up Parent Contacts So That They Will Be Positive When There Is a Problem to Discuss?

■ Always start a parent contact with something positive to say about the child.

■ Remember that the average parent will get a "thud" feeling in his or her stomach as soon as you say, "Hello, this is Janie's teacher." Don't take this personally. It probably comes from years of contact with teachers who forgot to make positive contacts about Janie. Alleviate this concern as soon as you identify yourself. Even if you are calling about a concern, immediately assure the parent that you know the problem can be solved and that you are willing to work hard to help.

■ Be sure you know about family situations so that you don't make a faux pas like calling Johnny Jones's mother Mrs. Jones if she is remarried and uses her second husband's name.

■ Go into a parent conference or call with concrete examples of the problem and what changes need to be made. The known is less scary than the unknown.

■ Plan out several ways that you intend to help solve the concern. Share these with the parent. Also, be sure you are ready with a response when the parent asks, "What can we do at home?" Make your solutions worthwhile and practical for the busy family.

- Remember that you and the parents are on the same team. You both want the child to be successful.
- Give or send the parent something written at the end of a phone or in-person conference. For instance, you might want to create a simple conference form.

Date of meeting: April 4

Main purpose of meeting: To help Jenny get her homework done and handed in.

Decisions: Jenny needs to be responsible for her homework, and we will help.

What the child needs to do: Jenny needs to write down her homework assignment in her notebook and be sure she brings home her books.

What the teacher will do: Ask Jenny if she has her notebook and books before she leaves the classroom.

Checking progress: After 2 weeks, we will talk about Jenny's progress and see if she can start to remember her homework and books without teacher reminders.

What the family will do: Buy Jenny a notebook. Ask her when she comes home what her homework is, and have her go back to school immediately to get her materials if she has forgotten them.

Figure 17.1. Parent-Teacher Conference Reminder

Try This Today

Just for a moment, imagine you have a child who is having problems in school. How would you want your child's teacher to approach a call or conference with you? Think about what the teacher might say and do to set you at ease, assure you of his or her support, and show concern for your child. Do that!

What Can I Do If a Parent Is Uncooperative?

- Listen! Many times, a parent feels that he or she has not been heard or understood. Let the parent talk first and get the frustration out of his or her system. When the emotion runs down, ask if you can share some thoughts and try to shift the tone from distress to positive action.
- If the parent has a history of being difficult, be even more prepared than you ordinarily would. Have your facts and suggestions lined up.
- Get the principal, a guidance counselor, or a team member to join you for the conference.
- Talk to the child's teachers from previous years to see what kind of advice they can offer.
- If the parent is not calm enough to be productive at a particular meeting, suggest scheduling another meeting for when he or she is better able to work on a solution.

Try This Today

No doubt, the administrator of your school has had hundreds of opportunities to deal with distressed parents. This is daily fare for principals. Take a moment to ask about a few approaches that he or she has found to be effective over the years. In addition to possibly getting a helpful idea or two that you can make your own, the administrator will feel good that you value his or her experience.

How Can I Keep in Touch With Parents Without Adding to My Already Hectic Schedule?

- Have a file of parent addresses and phone numbers on your desk so that you can quickly get this information.
- Make use of modern technology as much as possible. E-mail and phone answering machines make it possible for you to leave a quick message at a time that is convenient for you without getting tied up in a lengthy conversation when it is not needed.
- If you decide to send a newsletter, try to collaborate with other people at your grade level so that no one has to do all the work. Use some reprinted material and articles by the children. Keep the newsletter brief.

- Realize that the small amount of time you invest in a call may keep you from spending a lot more time later if a problem is permitted to develop.

- Let children and parent volunteers create some of your communications materials when you are simply passing on information about programs or needed materials.

- Set up a little corner of your room as a parent library. Try to find a spot near the door so that the materials are easily accessible without disturbing your class. Include books and articles that might help parents understand their children's development and your program. Let parents know that they can stop by and borrow materials at any time.

Try This Today

Keep notepaper handy on your desk so that you can grab a piece and jot down a note when you notice something you want to convey to a parent.

For More Ideas and Information . . .

- Read *Everybody's House—The Schoolhouse* by Carolyn Warner with Marilyn Curry (Corwin Press, 1-805-499-9734).

- Check out "The Parent Connection," a monthly newsletter in *Teaching K-8* magazine (1-800-678-8793).

- Use *Powerful Parent Letters for K-3* by Mary Anne Duggan (Corwin Press, 1-805-499-9734). And to make letter writing even easier, try *Notes Home: 115 Letters and Forms on CD-ROM for Busy Teachers,* also by Mary Anne Duggan and available from Corwin Press.

- Consider the ideas in *The Parent Project* by James Vopat (Stenhouse, 1-800-988-9812).

- Read *Parents on Your Side* by Lee Canter and Marlene Canter (Canter and Associates, 1-800-262-4347).

- Examine *How to Involve Parents in a Multicultural School* by Bruce Davis (Association for Supervision and Curriculum Development, 1-800-933-ASCD).

- Study *How to Deal With Parents Who Are Angry, Troubled, Afraid, or Just Plain Crazy* by Elaine K. McEwan (Corwin Press, 1-405-499-9734).

18

Getting Along With Administrators

Your relationship with your administrator has a big effect on how you feel about your job. It is worthwhile to get to know your administrator's philosophy, goals, and style so that you can appreciate the strengths that he or she brings to your school while learning how to navigate peacefully around any differences between the two of you.

What Do Administrators Expect From Teachers?

- Administrators expect their faculty members to make them look good! They want you to be part of the reason your school has an excellent reputation.

- They want you to provide a worthwhile program that fosters success with as many children as humanly possible.

- Being able to handle most of your students' behavior problems while knowing when a problem is serious enough for office involvement also endears you to your administrator.

- Your administrator expects you to communicate with parents in a way that builds harmony and minimizes misunderstanding and conflict.

- When you handle the mundane parts of teaching, such as getting paperwork in on time, without much grumbling, your administrator will be happy.

■ Getting along well with your colleagues and cultivating a team and school spirit makes you the kind of employee any administrator would love to have.

Try This Today

Showing sincere appreciation for what you see as your administrator's strengths is important. After all, administration is a hard job that often feels thankless. Pass on a compliment to your administrator.

What Kind of Support Can I Expect From My Administrator?

■ Your administrator should provide the materials you need within reason. His or her budgetary pockets are not limitless, but on the other hand, you should not be cutting into your salary check to buy the necessary tools of your trade.

■ You should be able to count on your administrator to defend you in parent and colleague disputes . . . when you have acted defensibly.

■ An administrator should be willing to "run interference" for you whenever possible to lessen the stress of red tape and district restrictions.

■ You should expect that your administrator will support you by talking to you directly and privately when he or she has a concern.

■ You should not expect your administrator to defend you when you have acted in error. An administrator cannot and should not say that you were right when you were not. It is hoped that he or she will help you examine what would have been a better course of action and do whatever possible to assist you in moving on from the mess you have created.

Try This Today

Think about any difficult situation you are currently handling with parents or children. Make it a point to see your administrator for a few minutes and update him or her on the situation and your plans for handling it. The administrator can support you much better and offer suggestions if he or she knows what is happening.

How Can I Handle the Situation If I Am Assigned to a School With an Administrator With Whom I Clash?

- Look closely at what disturbs you about your administrator. Nine times out of 10, what bothers you in another is some trait you actually possess that you do not like. (Don't you just hate that?)

- Try to get to know your administrator as a person. See if there is something you have in common, perhaps outside of education, that could be a foundation for better relations.

- If all this fails, remind yourself that this person is still your boss. Treat him or her with respect. Restrict complaining about the person to friends and family so that you don't fall into the trap of talking about the administrator with colleagues.

- Realize that sometimes styles don't mesh, and that does not mean that either person is wrong. If you are truly miserable, grin and bear it for the rest of the year while you try to lay the groundwork for a transfer.

- Explore a transfer by identifying schools that attract you for a particular reason so that you are going to something better rather than simply trying to escape from your current situation. When you must give a reason for your interest in a transfer, focus on positive reasons, not negative ones.

Try This Today

Step back and objectively chart, in your mind or on paper, the administrator's strengths and what you judge as weaknesses. Try to understand the weaknesses. Sometimes, understanding brings with it enough compassion to lower your stress level.

For More Ideas and Information . . .

- Read *Your Boss Is Not Your Mother* by Brian Des Roches (Avon Books, 1350 Avenue of the Americas, New York, NY 10019).

- Take a look at *People Styles at Work* by Robert Bolton and Dorothy Grover Bolton (AMACOM, American Management Association, 1601 Broadway, New York, NY 10019).

- Get *How Not to Take It Personally* by Vera M. Held (McGraw-Hill Ryerson, 300 Water Street, Whitby, Ontario, LIN 9B6).

19
Avoiding Burnout

Teaching is a demanding and complex job. It is easy to burn out early if you do not take definite steps to avoid it. The good news is that there are lots of ways to continue enjoying yourself while working hard.

What Are the Signs of Burnout?

- You could be headed toward burnout if you are spending all your "free" time or major chunks of it working on schoolwork.

- You are a likely candidate for burnout if you do not have an answer when people ask you about your hobbies, interests, and what you do for fun.

- You may be in the process of burning out if you notice your conversations with your colleagues are mostly "ain't it awful" exchanges instead of enthusiastic sharing of ideas about instructional strategies and ideas for motivating children.

- You could be suffering from burnout if you find yourself being out of school due to sickness a lot . . . even if you are really ill.

- You are surely a victim of burnout if you want to curl up in a ball and cry on Sunday night as you anticipate Monday morning.

 Try This Today

Notice the people around you today. Which seem burned out? Which seem full of enthusiasm for education? How can you tell? Think about which you resemble.

What Causes Burnout?

- You can burn out because teaching is not meeting your expectations, and you are not adjusting your expectations and realizing the difference between what you can and cannot control. For example, you know in your heart that parents should support the educational growth of their children, but the reality is that some cannot or will not.

- Burnout can be caused by being unrealistic about what you can accomplish. For example, you might want to send a personal note home to each child's parent every week. If you find this worthwhile goal very stressful because of lack of time and continue anyway rather than finding a more practical way to maintain parent contact, burnout is not far away.

- Not honoring the fact that you deserve time for yourself, your family, and your friends is a sure path to burnout.

- Working so hard that you make yourself literally sick and tired is a way to bring on burnout.

- Hanging around with colleagues who are negative rather than energetic and enthusiastic can hasten you along in a case of burnout.

Try This Today

See if you are in danger of burning out. At the end of each day for a few weeks, take a moment to put a smiley face or frowny face on the calendar to indicate how you felt about the school day. If lots of frownies are piling up, explore some ways to increase the smileys. See some suggestions in this section.

How Can I Avoid Burnout?

- Be realistic about what you can accomplish, and set about accomplishing it. Don't look back at what is impossible for you to address right now.

- Make some time for yourself every day. (Warning! A sign of burnout is looking at this suggestion and saying, "But I don't have time.") You can find at least 10 minutes to read an uplifting passage, take a walk around the block, or call a friend. Start recording these on your calendar to be sure you don't forget.

- Start a good news journal. Put a journal on your desk. At the end of each teaching day, write down three good things that happened that day to keep yourself focused on positive occurrences and accomplishments.
- Cultivate an outside interest if you do not already have one. Take a credit-free course, get a neighbor or two to commit to taking a daily walk with you after work, join a club, or do whatever interests you that has nothing to do with education. *Make* time to do this.

 Try This Today

Experiment with an alternative to having lunch in the teacher's lounge. If people who congregate there tend to complain a lot, consider taking your lunch outside and enjoying nature for a few minutes, or go to the room of a positive-minded teacher for your midday break. Notice how you feel.

What Can I Do If I Start to Feel Evidence of Burnout?

- Sit down with a piece of paper in a place where you won't be disturbed. List the parts of your job that you see as distressing. After you have gotten them all recorded, circle the ones over which you have some control. Jot notes beside them of what steps (even if they are little) you could take to improve the situation.
- Think of some things you could do to reignite your passion for education. Consider offering to present workshops, going to conferences, writing your teaching ideas for publication, or teaming with a colleague.
- Consider whether it is a time for a change of grade level, subject, or school to energize yourself.
- Talk to a therapist or counselor to process your feelings about your job, and brainstorm solutions. Don't hesitate. This kind of assistance is as accepted as going to see a medical doctor for a sore toe these days!
- Consider some alternative medicine options for stress management, such as biofeedback, acupuncture (it doesn't hurt), or massage. If you can handle your teaching with less stress, you will enjoy it more.

Try This Today

Seek out a veteran teacher on your faculty who is still enthusiastic about teaching. Have lunch, extend an invitation to go out for a cup of coffee after school, or approach the person to ask for ideas or advice about something you teach. Making contact with a person who has managed *not* to burn out can be rejuvenating.

For More Ideas and Information . . .

- Read *Time-Saving Tips for Teachers* by Joanne C. Strohmer and Clare Carhart (Corwin Press, 1-805-499-9734).

- Look at *Avoiding Burnout and Increasing Your Motivation* by Lee Canter and Marlene Canter (Canter and Associates, 1-800-262-4347).

- Read *Teachers Today: A Guide to Surviving Creatively* by Mary Zabolio McGrath (Corwin Press, 1-805-499-9734).

- Consider the ideas in *301 Ways to Have Fun at Work* by Dave Hemsath and Leslie Yerkes (Berrett-Koehler Publishers, 1-415-288-0260).

20
Serving on Committees

Getting involved in committee work can supercharge you . . . or drain you. Your feelings about this aspect of education depend on the decisions you make about how to approach these opportunities.

What Are the Pluses and Minuses of Volunteering for Committees?

- Committee work can keep you interested in education and encourage you to grow as you grapple with new challenges.

- Being involved in committees can help you see more of the big picture of education than you can see from your own classroom. Sometimes, this view can help you relieve stress by putting more energy into the aspects on which you can have an impact and letting go of the things beyond your control.

- Serving on a committee provides a change from your normal teaching routine.

- You can meet and network with new people while doing committee work.

- If there is a change that you think needs to be made in education, committee work can give you a platform to speak for that change.

- Committee work gives you something extra to put on your résumé.

- If you have questions about a particular aspect of instruction, serving on a committee focused on that topic may help you discover some new ideas.

- Committee work takes effort above and beyond your other teaching duties.

- Meetings associated with committees may require you to be out of the classroom; therefore, you have to prepare substitute plans.

- Committee work gives you an opportunity to learn new skills concerning dealing with egos . . . yours and theirs!

 Try This Today

Ask someone who serves on the kind of committee you think might interest you what they see as the rewarding and challenging aspects of that committee.

What Are the Secrets to Being a Productive Committee Member Without Becoming Overextended?

- Whenever possible, be selective about which committees you join. Try to predict how much "homework" a particular committee will require.

- Consider the important element of who is leading the committee. Is the chair someone with whom you can work well, or will you continually be rowing against the current?

- Be realistic when you are deciding how many times you can say yes when asked to serve on a committee. If you agree too many times, not only will the quality of your contributions to the committee suffer, but your classroom and home life could be affected as well.

- When you are serving on a particular committee, carefully weigh decisions about how many tasks you can take on or how many subcommittees you can join. It is okay to say, "I have hit my limit. I can't do any more without it affecting my main job—teaching."

- Know when you can make a difference by expressing your opinion about a committee issue and when you will do yourself and others a favor by refraining from comment.

- Be a committee member who is known for suggesting practical ideas that help solve problems rather than one who whines about "givens."

Try This Today

Be a productive member of the committee on which you are currently serving by sending a note to the chair expressing sincere appreciation for some aspect of how he or she is leading the group.

How Can I Back Out of Committees If I Feel a Need To?

- If you need to quit a committee because you are overextended, simply and honestly explain this to the chair and ask to be released.

- Back out with a positive attitude and grace. Do this even if you are leaving because you are distressed about some aspect of the committee's work. Leaving with hard feelings is never a good idea.

- If you enjoy the committee but are feeling stressed because of other school or home demands, consider leaving the door open for returning when your situation improves. You could simply ask the chair if you could take a leave of absence with the hope of rejoining the group.

Try This Today

Backing out of a committee actually boils down to using your "no" skills. Sharpen them by saying "no" . . . pleasantly . . . a few times when people ask something that would be an infringement on your time. Then, think how you could use your "no" skills to wiggle gracefully out of the committee.

For More Ideas and Information . . .

- Read *How to Get the Most out of Meetings* by Cindy Lakin Morley (Association for Supervision and Curriculum Development, 1-800-933-ASCD).

- Take a look at *How to Make Meetings Work* by Michael Doyle and David Straus (Jove, 200 Madison Avenue, New York, NY, 10016).

- Consider the ideas in *Rapid Problem Solving With Post-It Notes* by David Starker (Fisher Books, 1-520-744-6110).

21

Making the Most of Professional Development

Because you are devoting your life to working with young learners, it is important that you remain a lifelong learner. Whether you are involved in professional growth activities you have selected or ones you are required to attend, you can use effective strategies for making these experiences worthwhile.

What Kinds of Things Should I Do to Keep Advancing My Career?

- First, decide what "advance" means to you. Do you want to continue teaching and become the best teacher in your school? Do you have aspirations in administration? Determine your dreams so that you can make a professional development plan for making them come true.
- Take advantage of opportunities to attend conferences and workshops related to your particular interests.
- Keep a positive attitude about training imposed by your school or district. Even if attending a workshop on a particular topic would not be your choice, set yourself the goal of collecting at least three ideas to try out.

- Let your administrator and supervisors know about your special interests. Ask them to keep you in mind if they hear of organizations, materials, training, or people who might help you develop these areas.

- Join a professional organization related to your teaching interests. Become active in the group. Network with others who share your interests.

- Maintain a reasonable amount of professional reading. Select one or two journals to receive. Each month when they come, skim the table of contents and mark a few articles related to your special interests and talents. (Do not, however, be so unrealistic as to believe you can read the entire magazine every month.)

- Seek out colleagues who possess educational philosophies and interests that you admire. Consider getting together with them periodically, perhaps in a social setting such as a restaurant or someone's house, to discuss ideas and share materials.

 Try This Today

Write down your dream for your career in 5 years. Describe the details with as much specificity as you can. Keep this description in a place where you will see it often, for example, taped to the inside of your medicine chest or the inside cover of your plan book. Read it regularly to keep your vision fresh in your mind.

How Can I Fund These Endeavors?

- Your school administrator or district supervisor often has money to support attendance at workshops or conferences.

- Many school systems have a tuition reimbursement program. Check with the personnel office.

- Ask your administrator about starting a school professional library of books and journals, if one does not already exist. If this is not possible, perhaps colleagues would be willing to start one as a grassroots effort. Everyone, for example, could contribute books and journals they have already read to a designated bookshelf for borrowing.

- Sometimes, parent-teacher organizations will purchase materials that will be helpful to you and your colleagues if you can clearly explain how their children will ultimately benefit.

Try This Today

Write a note to someone in the grants department of your central office. Ask if there are grants available for professional development.

What Kind of Résumé and Portfolio Should I Build?

- Put your résumé on a computer now, even if you are not currently considering a new position. Once the information is on a computer, you can easily add to it as you go along. When a tempting opportunity comes to your attention, you will not be rushed in putting together this important document.

- Remember that a good résumé should be limited to two pages, be on high-quality paper, look totally professional, and be absolutely error free.

- Record the details of your regular teaching position, but especially be on the lookout for what makes you stand out from the crowd. If nothing does, find an area of specialty and develop it.

- Although you will have your basic résumé saved on your computer, you will want to tailor the slant to the specific position for which you are applying. Use "save as" to create special versions of your résumé, and then keep these for future reference, too.

- Be aware that a portfolio can be an impressive aid when trying to get a new position.

- Divide your portfolio into sections with tabs. Be sure that every piece you put in it is easy to comprehend at a glance, because that is all the attention it may get. Use visuals whenever appropriate. Point out important parts using a highlighter.

- Your portfolio can be used in end-of-the-year evaluations on your current job even if you are not considering applying for a new position.

Try This Today

Be conscious of saving artifacts for your portfolio. As you put together especially creative and effective lessons, save a copy for your portfolio. Also, be aware of photo opportunities related to your classroom decor and activities. Start a folder for artifacts, and put at least one thing in it today.

How Do I Know When I Should Look for a New Position?

■ When you start to feel that you have your job "down to a tee," consider whether you should seek a new one to avoid getting bored. You might want to continue to teach but change grade levels, subject areas if you are departmentalized, or schools.

■ If you have finished a degree that qualifies you for a new position, such as special educator or reading specialist, and you are itching to try your new ideas, consider your options.

■ Perhaps you are starting to feel drawn to the idea of sharing your ideas with a larger audience. In that case, you might ponder the possibilities of applying for administrative or staff development positions for which you are qualified.

■ If there is someone, such as an administrator, from whom you think you could learn a lot, consider applying for an opening that would allow you to work with him or her.

 Try This Today

On a piece of scrap paper, make a column on the left side. Write the following in the column from top to bottom: next year, 2 years from now, 5 years from now, 10 years from now, retirement. On the right-hand side, across from each phrase, write the feeling that comes to mind when you think of being in your current job at each of those points. If words like desperate, trapped, and frustrated are coming up near the top of the list, get busy checking out other options. Your work is supposed to be joyful and enriching. Don't settle for less for too long.

How Can I Go About Exploring My Options?

■ The best way to explore your options is to consider your contacts. If you don't have any, cultivate some. It is what you know *and* who you know that count.

- Let your contacts (administrators with whom you have a positive relationship, well-respected teachers, supervisors, and others) know of your interest in expanding your horizons.
- Be sure your supervisor and principal know of your intentions first so that they don't hear from others. Stress that you are happy where you are and would be glad to continue. Explain that your goal is to keep fresh by exploring future challenges to keep growing.

Try This Today

Talk to someone outside your school system, such as an education professor or an administrator in another district, about what kinds of options you have. Discuss your current background and what else you might need to acquire. This approach allows you to seek information about possibilities in the early stages without notifying colleagues or your administrator before you are ready to make any moves.

For More Ideas and Information . . .

- Select articles from *Phi Delta Kappan* (1-800-766-1156) and *Educational Leadership* (1-800-933-2723) to keep up with the big issues in education.
- Use *Teacher Self-Evaluation Tool Kit* by Peter W. Airasian and Arlene Gullickson (Corwin Press, 1-805-499-9734).
- Get some ASCD Select topics, which include articles and abstracts on a wide variety of topics (Association for Supervision and Curriculum Development, 1-800-933-ASCD).
- Read the "Professional Growth" columns in *Teaching K-8* magazine (1-800-678-8793).

22

Presenting at Faculty Meetings or Conferences

You have a lot to share with colleagues. The particular combinations of youngsters you have taught and your unique philosophy and style ensure that you have learned some things that others could profit from knowing. Presenting may sound scary at first, but it can be fun and rewarding.

How Can I "Break Into" Presenting?

- Let people know that you are willing to present. For instance, you could take a deep breath and say to your principal or district supervisor, "Last week, you complimented me on how well my writing workshop is working. I would be glad to share those ideas at a faculty meeting (or district training session) sometime."

- Offer to co-present with a colleague who presents on a topic that is complementary to some of your areas of expertise. For example, if you have a friend who offers workshops on integrated instruction, you might offer to share your successful integrated unit during his or her next presentation.

- If you are in a meeting with people from other schools or other districts who express interest in your teaching ideas, tell them you would be glad to do a presentation for them sometime.

- Be on the lookout for local, state, or national conferences that accept proposals for presentations.

Try This Today

Pick out a unit, lesson, or activity that has worked particularly well. Send it to someone who is responsible for staff development in your system. Attach a little note explaining how well this idea has worked, and say that you are willing to share the idea with other teachers.

What Kinds of Ideas Could I Present?

- Teachers always love to hear about practical, effective ideas that work. Simple presentations on lessons, projects, and units that have worked appeal to audiences.
- Share how you have adapted techniques devised by other educators. This could involve adaptations of textbook materials or approaches such as reader's theater.
- Show how you have managed to streamline particular teaching responsibilities so that you can stay sane while still offering an exemplary program for youngsters.
- Offer teacher audiences a chance to learn or practice a new skill, such as taking a running record or using a particular computer program.

Try This Today

Start a notebook of presentation topics. You may want to use a separate page for each topic that occurs to you. This approach will give you room to list or mind-map what you might cover in relation to the topic. Whenever you think of a presentation topic idea, jot it in your notebook.

How Can I Organize My Ideas Into a Presentation?

- Use the same good teaching practices you use with children.
- Be sure to avoid "talking at" your audience the entire time. Intersperse activity with your explanations. You can provide time for the audience to try out ideas or engage in a brief think-pair-share activity in response to what you have presented.

- Be sure to build in breaks if your presentation is much over an hour long. Adults have as much trouble sitting still for extended periods of time as youngsters.

- Plan your timing carefully. The worst thing that can happen to a presenter is to finish an hour-long presentation in 10 minutes. (Trust me. It happened to me, and I still blush when I think of it!) The second worst thing is to prepare so much that you rush through breathlessly. Plan the main part of your presentation. Then, go back and mark on your notes what you can leave out if you are running out of time. Also, insert notes about some places you can expand, or create a few worthwhile activities that would make sense at the end of your session, if needed.

- Remember that almost nothing starts on time. Be prepared for the possibility of having less time than you have been told you will have.

- Run through your presentation *aloud* several times when you are at home alone. Actually speaking the words helps you to know where you might stumble or what sounds awkward. Of course, this rehearsal also provides you with a check on timing. Remember, however, that the actual presentation will take longer than your at-home run-through.

- An overhead projector is a presenter's best friend. Transparencies not only help visual learners in your audience but also provide notes from which you can speak. (Check out the working condition and position of the equipment before your audience arrives.)

 Try This Today

See if a planning chart like this sample one is helpful to you.

TABLE 22.1   Presentation Planning Format

Concepts to Get Across	Approach	Materials	Time
Overview of process writing	Overhead transparency	Overhead	10 minutes
Description of each stage	Project with teachers doing each stage with their own topics	Prewriting Peer revision sheets Editing sheet	30 minutes
Reaction to the process	Group discussion		15 minutes

What Should I Keep in Mind While I Am Presenting?

- Present with a twinkle in your eye. Your enthusiasm will be as contagious with adults as it is with children.

- Do not start with an apology. For example, you lose the audience immediately if you say, "I did not really have time to prepare . . ." They could logically ask, "Why not? Weren't we important enough to you?"

- Remember to honor the experience and expertise of your audience. Even though you are the one who is on stage, members of your audience probably also have ideas to share relative to the topic.

- Active involvement does not mean that you should have the audience pretend they are children. This can be embarrassing to many.

- If you want your audience to experience a particular instructional technique, have them try it out with material at their learning level. For example, if you wanted an audience to experience what it is like to be a struggling reader, give them a chance to read a piece from an advanced chemistry text.

- The audience's empathy is generally with you. They want you to be successful because they can imagine what it would feel like if they were the ones on stage.

- Paraphrase ideas from overhead transparencies or handouts, adding little tidbits and examples, if you need to go over these as part of your presentation. Avoid, however, reading the material to your audience, or they can fairly ask, "Why didn't she (he) just send this to me instead of taking up my time sitting here? I can read!"

- Be sensitive to the middle-aged folks in your audience. It is frustrating to try to read 12-point type on an overhead transparency screen. Use at least 14-point bold. Larger font sizes are even better.

 Try This Today

The next time you are in the audience when an educator is presenting, note what works and what does not. In addition to taking notes on the content of the session, use a separate sheet to record thoughts about presentation style and techniques.

For More Ideas and Information . . .

- Read *13 Proven Ways to Get Your Message Across* by Ernest Brewer (Corwin Press, 1-805-499-9734).

- Look for ideas in *How to Make Presentations That Teach and Transform* by Robert Garmston and Bruce Wellman (Association for Supervision and Curriculum Development, 1-800-933-ASCD).

- Check out *Making Presentations With Confidence* by Vivian Buchan (Barron's, 250 Wireless Boulevard, Hauppauge, NY 11788).

- Consider the ideas in *Power Presentations* by Marjorie Brody and Shawn Kent (John Wiley).

23

Interviewing for a New Position

The time may come when you feel challenged by the idea of trying a new role, such as that of a specialist or administrator, or you simply want to change grades or schools to keep yourself motivated. Chances are you may feel confident in your ability to do the job for which you are applying but feel a little rusty in the area of job interview skills. With a little planning, you can have a great interview and enhance your chances of getting the position you wish.

How Can I Get an Interview?

- It is not enough to apply for the job you want by contacting the personnel department. Make direct contact with the person who will do the hiring by sending a copy of your résumé with a carefully written cover letter.

- Send sample materials, such as an exemplary lesson plan you have created, to the person who will be hiring.

- If you are interested in being informed about a particular type of position when it becomes open, stay in contact with the relevant administrator. From time to time, send a polite, cheerful note reminding him or her of your interest in a position.

- Think of any contacts you have. Ask them to speak about your experience and the quality of your work to the person who will be hiring.

Try This Today

List everyone you can think of who might be a contact or impressive reference. Pick out one to call today.

How Should I Prepare for an Interview?

- Do your homework!
- Try to predict the questions you will be asked. Jot down notes about the points you would want to make in your response.
- Prepare a portfolio. Include information that can be taken in at a glance, such as snapshots of your classroom and special projects, lesson plans with important parts highlighted, or graphic organizers showing how you would organize and implement a program.
- Talk to a person who is in a role similar to that of the person who will interview you. Ask his or her opinion about what will be important to a successful interview.
- Discuss your upcoming interview with someone who is in the role you are applying to fill. See what tips you can get.

Try This Today

Take a risk. Talk to someone you trust who knows you well. Ask him or her to tell you what you need to be aware of in order to put forth your best foot. For example, this friend or family member might be able to gently remind you to avoid being so humble that the interviewer doesn't know your strengths or to stick to the question and answer succinctly if you have a tiny tendency to ramble.

What Should I Be Aware of During the Interview?

- Your job in the interview is to show what you know.
- After talking with you, the interviewer will need to feel confident that you have a good base of information and that your philosophy is reasonably in line with his or hers. It is okay that you do not know everything, but you

need to come across as someone who has the intelligence and initiative to learn quickly.

- The interviewer wants to see who you are as well as what you know. Keep your professional demeanor while you also let your personality come through.

- Strike a balance between not wanting to drone on and being sure you provide enough detail. One of the biggest mistakes that interviewees make is not providing enough detail in their responses.

- Do not hesitate to take notes while you listen to the interview questions. This practice can help you remember all the parts and directly respond to the questions rather than rambling. Straying from the topic can make you sound like you do not have an answer or that you are trying to avoid the question.

- Think ahead about how you can use your portfolio during the interview to illustrate points as you go along. Do not simply pull it out at the end of the meeting when it may not get the attention it deserves.

 Try This Today

Whether it seems fair or not, appearances do have an influence over people. You will need to dress the part of a professional even if you are interviewing with someone you know well. Look in your closet to see if you have an outfit you could wear with confidence if an interview were to suddenly come your way.

What If I Don't Get the Job?

- Realize that not getting the job may not necessarily mean there was a problem with you. It may mean that a different personality or kind of experience was needed to round out the team. For example, maybe all the other teachers at the grade level were very global thinkers like you, and the principal felt that a more analytic thinker was needed to provide balance.

- Ask for feedback from the interviewer. Do this in a positive, professional manner. Simply say that you would appreciate one or two suggestions so that you can improve the next time you interview for a position. Genuinely thank the person for the input.

- Decide on some ways you can strengthen your background even more. Figure a way to stand out from the crowd. For instance, you may want to start presenting workshops or writing articles to show that you have that something extra.

- Send a thank-you note to the person who interviewed you. Mention that you are interested in future positions that become available.

Try This Today

Try, try again. Give yourself a *short* period of time to recover from the disappointment . . . and even feel sorry for yourself . . . and then get out there and continue looking for the right position with as much enthusiasm as ever.

For More Ideas and Information . . .

- Read *101 Grade A Resumes for Teachers* by Rebecca Anthony and Gerard Roe (Barron's).

- Study *Job Interviews for Dummies* by Joyce Lain Kennedy (IDG Books, 1-800-762-2974).

- Read *From Contact to Contract* by Rebecca Anthony and Gerard Roe (Sulzberger).

- Take a look at *How to Get a Job in Education* by Joel Levin (Adams).

24
Relax!

If you have committed to sweating the important small stuff, you can relax now and enjoy your teaching program more than ever before. Sweating the key details is an insurance policy that will result in your major catastrophe quotient going way down. Your new mental set will be one of preventing problems before they happen and finding the smoothest possible route to your instructional objectives.

As you sweat the small stuff in order to lower your stress level in your professional life, consider using the extra time and energy you are generating to nurture yourself. Sweating the small stuff on the job should make it possible for you to have a more peaceful mind, a more enthusiastic feeling about teaching, and more time to spend on personal pursuits that enrich your life and with the family and friends who are dear to you. So sweat the small stuff and then enjoy!

CORWIN
PRESS

The Corwin Press logo—a raven striding across an open book—represents the happy union of courage and learning. We are a professional-level publisher of books and journals for K–12 educators, and we are committed to creating and providing resources that embody these qualities. Corwin's motto is "Success for All Learners."